# Survey of College Students 2025, Use of Generative Artificial Intelligence



 ISBN 979-8-88517-279-0

## Table of contents

## THE QUESTIONNAIRE

1. Please fill in the following contact information. If you win the drawing your Amazon card will be sent to this email address.

    A. Name:
    B. Name of College that You Attend:
    C. Email Address

2. How old are you? (answer in number of years) e.g., "19" Or "23"
Do not include fractions or descriptive phrases such as "years old"

3. Choose the phrase which best describes where you grew up before you went to college. If more than one answer applies to you, choose the one that you feel best reflects who you believe that you are.

    A. I grew up in a major city with more than 350,000 people
    B. I grew up in a small or medium sized city with less than 350,000 people.
    C. I grew up in a suburban area
    D. I grew up in a rural area.

4. I grew up mostly in:

    A. The South
    B. The Northeast
    C. The Midwest
    D. The West
    E. in Canada
    F. Abroad (other than Canada)

5. This semester I am a:

    A. First Year Student
    B. Sophomore
    C. Junior
    D. Senior

6. The approximate annual income level of my family of origin (your Mom & Dad or legal guardian) was. For students over the age of 40 use your current family income.

    A. Less than $50,000 per year
    B. $50,000 to $90,000 per year
    C. $90,000+ to $150,000 per year
    D. $150,000+ to $250,000 per year
    E. More than $250,000 per year

7. How would you describe your relationship with organized religion?

A. I practice a religion thoroughly and consider my religion to be a very important part of my life.
B. I practice a religion and try to attend regular services and to participate as much as I can.
C. I identify with a religion but can't say I put a lot of effort into practicing it.
D. I don't really believe in or practice an organized religion.

8. Choose the phrase that best describes your political views:

A. Very Left Wing
B. Liberal
C. Middle of the Road
D. Conservative
E. Very Right Wing

9. Which phrase best describes your college academic performance? (If you have not yet received any grades, choose what your tests and other experiences suggest will be your grades)

A. A or A- average or more
B. B or B+ average
C. C or C+ average
D. D or D+ average or less

10. Choose the phrase that best describes your academic major or likely major:

A. Business, Economics or Finance
B. Fine Arts and Architecture
C. Music, Dance, Theater, other Performing Arts
D. English, Foreign Languages, Comp Literature, Creative Writing
E. Biology, Physics, Chemistry, Pre-Med
F. Geology, Oceanography, Environmental Sciences
G. Engineering, Mathematics, Computer Science
H. Philosophy, Theology
I. History, Classics
J. Sociology, Political Science, Anthropology or other Social Science, except Economics and Psychology
K. Psychology
L. Education or Library Science
M. Criminology/Law Enforcement
N. Occupational or Physical Therapy, Nursing, Public Health, Nutrition. other Health-Related
O. Communications, Media, Journalism
P. Other (please specify)

11. You are:

    A. Male
    B. Female
    C. Transgender

12. Currently you live:

    A. At home with my parents or guardian
    B. Off campus with others who are not my parents or guardian
    C. Off campus alone
    D. In fraternity or sorority supplied housing
    E. On campus in the dorms or college-provided suites

13. Which phrase best describes your current employment situation:

    A. I don't have a full or part time job.
    B. I have a part time job.
    C. I have a full time job.

14. Which phrase best describes your sexual orientation?

    A. Heterosexual or "straight"
    B. Homosexual or "gay"
    C. Bi-sexual

15. Which category best captures your highest overall SAT or ACT score? The SAT score is based on the new 1600 point standard so if you were tested under the old 2400 point standard it would be 2/3 of this score.

    A. 30 or over ACT or 1350 or over SAT
    B. 24-29 ACT or 1170 to 1349 SAT
    C. 20-23 ACT or 1050 to 1169 SAT
    D. 17-19 ACT or 900 to 1050 SAT
    E. 16 or Under ACT or Under 900 SAT
    F. Never Took Either Test

16. Which phrase best describes your racial or ethnic identity?

    A. White or Caucasian
    B. Black or African American
    C. Latino or Hispanic
    D. Asian or Asian American
    E. American Indigenous, Eskimo, Pacific Islander, Hawaiian Native
    F. Mixed Race

17. Which phrase best approximates your religion and, if you have or do not identify with a religion, please choose choice 1.

A. I do not practice or identify with an organized religion
B. Catholic
C. Lutheran
D. Baptist
E. Evangelical Protestant Christianity
F. Protestant Christianity
G. Orthodox Christianity
H. Buddhism
I. Non-Denominational Christianity
J. Hinduism
K. Islam
L. Judaism
M. Sikhism
N. Other (please specify)

18. Which of the following have you used in the past month? (check all that apply)

A. Microsoft CoPilot
B. ChatGPT (any version)
C. Gemini
D. Claude
E. Midjourney
F. Grok
G. Other (please specify)

19. In the past week how much time, in minutes, have you spent using the artificial intelligence applications listed below, or similar such applications?

A. ChatGPT
B. Gemini
C. CoPilot
D. Midjourney
E. Claude
F. All Other AI Generative Applications

20. About how important is it to you to learn to use generative artificial intelligence applications effectively?

A. Not at all important
B. Not too important
C. Somewhat important
D. Important
E. Very Important

21. Do you have a paid subscription to ChatGPT?

A. Yes
B. No
C. If so, identify this application

22. Do you have a personal paid subscription to any other generative AI application other than ChatGPT?

A. Yes
B. No

23. What do you primarily use artificial intelligence applications for?

24. When you conduct general internet searches, about what percentage of the time do you use a generative AI application to accompany or fully replace your usual search engine?

## Characteristics of the sample

Age of respondent

| | # |
|---|---|
| Less than 19 | 379 |
| 19-21 | 238 |
| 22-27 | 211 |
| Over 28 | 194 |
| Total | 1022 |

Urban, suburban or rural upbringing

| | # |
|---|---|
| I grew up in a major city with more than 350,000 people | 264 |
| I grew up in a small or medium sized city with less than 350,000 people. | 254 |
| I grew up in a suburban area | 318 |
| I grew up in a rural area. | 180 |
| Unknown | 6 |
| Total | 1022 |

Region of upbringing

| | # |
|---|---|
| The South | 245 |
| The Northeast | 90 |
| The Midwest | 398 |
| The West | 118 |
| Abroad | 164 |
| Unknown | 7 |
| Total | 1022 |

Year of class standing

| | # |
|---|---|
| First year student | 397 |
| Sophomore | 180 |
| Junior | 171 |
| Senior | 258 |
| Unknown | 16 |
| Total | 1022 |

Annual family of origin income level

| | # |
|---|---|
| Less than $50,000 per year | 314 |
| $50,000 to $90,000 per year | 294 |
| $90,000+ to $150,000 per year | 198 |
| $150,000+ to $250,000 per year | 104 |
| More than $250,000 per year | 90 |
| Unknown | 22 |
| Total | 1022 |

Relationship with organized religion

| | # |
|---|---|
| I practice a religion thoroughly and consider my religion to be a very important part of my life. | 196 |
| I practice a religion and try to attend regular services and to participate as much as I can. | 157 |
| I identify with a religion but can't say I put a lot of effort into practicing it. | 274 |
| I don't really believe in or practice an organized religion. | 387 |
| Unknown | 8 |
| Total | 1022 |

Political views

| | # |
|---|---|
| Very left wing | 151 |
| Liberal | 369 |
| Middle of the road | 335 |
| Conservative | 138 |
| Very right wing | 20 |
| Unknown | 9 |
| Total | 1022 |

College grades

| | # |
|---|---|
| A or A- average or more | 655 |
| B or B+ average | 301 |
| C or C+ or lower | 62 |
| Unknown | 4 |
| Total | 1022 |

Academic major

| | # |
|---|---|
| Business, Economics or Finance | 126 |
| Fine Arts and Architecture | 63 |
| Music, Dance, Theater, other Performing Arts | 26 |
| English, Foreign Languages, Comp Literature, Creative Writing | 29 |
| Biology, Physics, Chemistry, Pre-Med | 133 |
| Geology, Oceanography, Environmental Sciences | 26 |
| Engineering, Mathematics, Computer Science | 202 |
| History, Classics | 13 |
| Sociology, Political Science, Anthropology or other Social Science, except Economics and Psychology | 76 |
| Psychology | 94 |
| Education or Library Science | 74 |
| Criminology/Law Enforcement | 15 |
| Occupational or Physical Therapy, Nursing, Public Health, Nutrition. other Health-Related | 108 |
| Communications, Media, Journalism | 24 |
| Other | 13 |
| Total | 1022 |

Gender of respondent

| | # |
|---|---|
| Male | 342 |
| Female | 620 |
| Transgender | 57 |
| Unknown | 3 |
| Total | 1022 |

Status of current residency

| | # |
|---|---|
| At home with my parents or guardian | 221 |
| Off campus with others who are not my parents or guardian | 252 |
| Off campus alone | 115 |
| On campus in the dorms or college-provided suites | 431 |
| Unknown | 3 |
| Total | 1022 |

Current employment situation

| | # |
|---|---|
| I don't have a full or part time job. | 414 |
| I have a part time job. | 450 |
| I have a full time job. | 152 |
| Unknown | 6 |
| Total | 1022 |

Sexual orientation

| | # |
|---|---|
| Heterosexual or "straight" | 719 |
| Homosexual or "gay" | 74 |
| Bi-sexual | 214 |
| Unknown | 15 |
| Total | 1022 |

SAT or ACT score

| | # |
|---|---|
| 30 or over ACT or 1350 or over SAT | 251 |
| 24-29 ACT or 1170 to 1349 SAT | 257 |
| 20-23 ACT or 1050 to 1169 SAT | 180 |
| 17-19 ACT or 900 to 1050 SAT | 88 |
| 16 or Under ACT or Under 900 SAT | 27 |
| Never took either test | 208 |
| Unknown | 11 |
| Total | 1022 |

Race or ethnicity

| | # |
|---|---|
| White or Caucasian | 519 |
| Black or African American | 133 |
| Latino or Hispanic | 104 |
| Asian or Asian American | 178 |
| American Indigenous, Eskimo, Pacific Islander, Hawaiian Native | 5 |
| Mixed race | 71 |
| Unknown | 12 |
| Total | 1022 |

Religion

| | # |
|---|---|
| I do not practice or identify with an organized religion | 381 |
| Catholic | 135 |
| Lutheran | 32 |
| Baptist | 63 |
| Evangelical Protestant Christianity | 23 |
| Protestant Christianity | 50 |
| Orthodox Christianity | 18 |
| Buddhism | 20 |
| Non-Denominational Christianity | 111 |
| Hinduism | 50 |
| Islam | 48 |
| Judaism | 27 |
| Mormon | 6 |
| Other | 58 |
| Total | 1022 |

Public or private college

| | # |
|---|---|
| Public | 788 |
| Private | 234 |
| Total | 1022 |

Enrollment of college attended

| | # |
|---|---|
| Less than 5,000 | 252 |
| 5,000+ - 12,000 | 260 |
| 12,000+ - 22,900 | 234 |
| More than 22,900 | 276 |
| Total | 1022 |

Tuition of college attended

| | # |
|---|---|
| Less than $6,000 | 267 |
| $6,000+ - $12,000 | 246 |
| $12,000+ - $20,000 | 262 |
| More than $20,000 | 247 |
| Total | 1022 |

# SUMMARY OF MAIN FINDINGS

## Overall AI Usage Trends

- ChatGPT is the most widely used AI tool among students, with 64.77% of the sample having used it in the past month.
- Microsoft CoPilot and Gemini have been used by 15.46% and 13.60% of students, respectively.
- Claude (5.77%), Midjourney (1.66%), and Grok (0.98%) have relatively low adoption.
- A variety of other AI tools (e.g., Grammarly, Adobe Firefly, Perplexity AI, Snapchat AI) were also mentioned in open responses, but their usage was sporadic.

---

## Generative AI Usage Patterns by Demographics and Institutional Factors

### By Tuition and Enrollment

- ChatGPT is more popular at higher-tuition institutions (79.35% usage at colleges with tuition above $20,000 vs. 53.93% at those under $6,000).
- Microsoft CoPilot is slightly more popular among students attending mid-range tuition colleges ($12,000–$20,000: 20.23%), while those in the highest tuition category use it less (10.93%).
- AI usage trends higher at smaller colleges for ChatGPT (76.19% at colleges with fewer than 5,000 students) and mid-sized colleges for CoPilot (peaking at 19.62% for schools with 5,000–12,000 students).

### Public vs. Private Colleges

- ChatGPT is more widely used at private colleges (77.35% vs. 61.04% at public colleges).
- Conversely, Microsoft CoPilot usage is higher at public colleges (16.88% vs. 10.68% at private colleges).
- Gemini use was fairly evenly split (13.83% at public and 12.82% at private colleges)

### By Age Group

- ChatGPT usage is consistent across age groups (62%–68%), showing broad appeal.
- Microsoft CoPilot sees slightly higher adoption among older students (22+ years), with 18.48% usage among 22-27-year-olds vs. 12.93% for those under 19.

### By Region and Upbringing

- ChatGPT is most popular among students raised abroad (81.10%) and in the West (76.27%), while Microsoft CoPilot is more common among those from major cities (18.18%).
- Rural students use ChatGPT less (57.22%)
- Use of Gemini was highest among those in major cities (16.29%).

### By Class Standing

- Seniors use AI tools slightly more than first-year students:
    - ChatGPT usage increases to 69.77% in senior year.
    - Microsoft CoPilot usage is highest among seniors (17.05%) and slightly lower in the earlier years.
    - Gemini use is also highest among seniors (15.5%),

---

### By Family Income

- ChatGPT usage is highest among high-income students ($150,000–$250,000: 71.15%) but remains strong across all income levels.
- Microsoft CoPilot is most used by students from low-income backgrounds (<$50,000: 20.38%) and least used by those from wealthier families (10.00% for $250,000+).
- Gemini use was also highest among those with the lowest incomes (17.2%).

### By Employment Status & Living Situation

- Students living off-campus alone are more likely to use Microsoft CoPilot (21.74%) and ChatGPT (63.48%).
- Full-time workers use Microsoft CoPilot more (19.08%) than part-time workers (13.56%).
- ChatGPT usage is lowest among full-time workers (54.61%), likely due to work obligations.

---

### By Academic Performance (Grades & SAT/ACT Scores)

- Students with A- or higher GPAs use ChatGPT the most (67.18%), with usage dropping among students with lower grades.
- Microsoft CoPilot usage is fairly uniform across grade levels.
- Students who never took the SAT/ACT use ChatGPT at a high rate (70.19%), potentially indicating a correlation with alternative educational pathways.
- Gemini use was highest among those in the two highest SAT/ACT bands.

### By Major

- ChatGPT usage is highest among Engineering/Computer Science students (77.72%) and Business majors (73.02%).
- Microsoft CoPilot is most used in Engineering (26.24%) and Criminology/Law Enforcement (26.67%).
- Similarly Gemini use was highest in STEM areas (22.77% for Engineering/Mathematics, Computer Science).
- Fine Arts, English, and Social Sciences students are the least likely to use AI tools.

### By Gender

- Male students use AI tools at significantly higher rates than females:
  - ChatGPT: 73.98% males vs. 61.61% females.
  - Microsoft CoPilot: 22.81% males vs. 12.42% females.
  - Gemini: 19.59% for males, 10.32% for females.

### By Religion

- Hindu students have the highest ChatGPT (72%), Gemini (34%) and Microsoft CoPilot (36%) usage.
- Catholic and Protestant students have above-average AI usage.
- Jewish students have low adoption (3.70% use Microsoft CoPilot and 66.67% use ChatGPT).

### By Political Ideology

- Middle-of-the-road and liberal students use ChatGPT more (~69%) than those who are very left-wing (52%).
- Microsoft CoPilot is more common among middle-of-the-road and conservative students (~19%) than liberals (10.57%).

---

## Key Takeaways

1. ChatGPT dominates AI adoption among college students, whereas Microsoft CoPilot and Gemini have niche audiences.
2. Students at higher-tuition and private institutions use AI more frequently.
3. Technical majors (engineering, business, and computer science) are the biggest AI adopters.
4. Socioeconomic status plays a role, with higher-income students using AI more, except for Microsoft CoPilot, which is more popular among lower-income students.
5. Males, older students, and students from major cities are more likely to use AI.
6. Religious and political identity affect AI use, with more engagement among Hindus and political moderates.

## Summary of Key Findings on AI Application Usage and Importance of Learning AI Skills

### 1. Time Spent Using ChatGPT

- ChatGPT had the highest average usage, with a mean of 34.99 minutes per week, though the median was 0 minutes, indicating a strong skew with some users using it heavily while others not at all.
- Usage varied significantly by demographic factors:
  - Students at institutions with tuition between $6,000 and $12,000 reported the highest mean usage (46.44 minutes).
  - Private college students (46.67minutes) reported higher mean usage than private college students (31.58 minutes).
  - By age group, younger students (ages 19-21) showed the highest usage (47.66 minutes mean).
  - Psychology majors (62.6) spent more time on ChatGPT compared to those studying other disciplines.

### Time Spent Using Applications Other than ChatGPT

  - Gemini: 4.84 minutes mean
  - CoPilot: 4.02 minutes mean
  - Midjourney: 0.47 minutes mean
  - Claude: 1.29 minutes mean
  - All Other Generative AI Applications: 3.23 minutes mean

### Self-Assessment of Importance of Learning AI

- 59.24% of students considered learning generative AI "somewhat important" to "very important."
- 34.35% of students expressed lower levels of interest ("not at all important" or "not too important").
- Demographic trends in AI learning interest:
  - Private college students (23.08% "important" and 14.10% "very important") valued AI skills more than public college students.
  - Students with family incomes over $150,000 were more likely to find AI important.
  - STEM students, especially Engineering, Math, and Computer Science majors (26.24% "important," 17.33% "very important"), expressed stronger interest.
  - Students who identified as "very right-wing" (35% important/very important) had more interest in AI than those identifying as "very left-wing" (only 19.86%).
  - Students at medium-sized colleges (5,000–12,000 students) showed the highest interest (35% "somewhat important" or higher).
  - Students who live off-campus alone (22.61% "important," 15.65% "very important") were more likely to value AI learning.
  - LGBTQ+ students (especially transgender and bisexual students) showed lower interest than heterosexual students in AI learning.

## Key Demographic Disparities in College Student AI Usage

- AI usage was highly uneven across demographic and institutional factors.
- Students with higher grades (B or better) were more likely to use ChatGPT.
- Higher-income students were less likely to use AI tools regularly but were more interested in learning how to use them effectively.
- Race and ethnicity showed significant gaps, with Black students using ChatGPT far more than White or Asian students.
- Religious students who regularly practice were more likely to spend time using ChatGPT (302.15 minutes mean).
- Political views influenced AI usage and learning interest, with liberals using ChatGPT more but conservatives more interested in learning AI.

## Conclusion

- While ChatGPT is the dominant AI tool among college students, most students spend little to no time using other AI tools.
- AI learning interest is moderate but varies widely by demographics, college type, and personal background.
- There is a strong divide between power users and non-users, with some students logging extensive time while others avoid AI tools entirely.
- The role of AI in higher education is growing, but major disparities remain in who uses AI and who wants to learn more about it.

## Key Findings on Paid Subscriptions to ChatGPT and Generative AI Usage

### Paid Subscription to ChatGPT

- 8.12% of students reported having a paid subscription to ChatGPT, while 83.66% did not.
- Higher tuition colleges had a higher percentage of paid subscribers, with students at institutions charging over $20,000 in tuition reporting the highest rate (13.36%).
- Students at smaller colleges (<5,000 enrollment) were more likely to have a subscription (11.90%), while those at large colleges (22,900+ enrollment) had the lowest (5.80%).
- Private college students (13.25%) were more than twice as likely to pay for ChatGPT than public college students (6.60%).
- Older students (28+) had the highest subscription rates (14.43%), while younger students (under 19) had the lowest (3.96%).
- Urban students were more likely to have a paid subscription (10.61%) compared to rural students (5.56%).
- Regional differences were notable, with students from abroad (20.12%) being the most likely to pay for ChatGPT.
- Seniors were the most likely to have a subscription (14.73%), compared to first-year students (5.04%).
- Students from high-income families ($150,000–$250,000) were most likely to pay for ChatGPT (16.35%), but those from families making less than $50,000 also had a relatively high subscription rate (11.15%).

- Political alignment played a role, with "very right-wing" students having the highest subscription rate (15.00%).
- STEM students (especially Engineering, Math, and Computer Science at 14.85%) had the highest rates of ChatGPT subscriptions, while majors like History (0%) and Fine Arts (1.59%) had the lowest.
- Males (13.16%) were significantly more likely than females (5.65%) to have a paid subscription.
- Students living off-campus alone were the most likely to pay for ChatGPT (15.65%), while those living at home with parents had lower rates (5.43%).
- Employment did not strongly correlate with ChatGPT subscriptions, with part-time and unemployed students having similar rates (~7-9%).
- Asian origin students (14.61%) were the most likely to pay for ChatGPT, while Black students had one of the lowest rates (4.51%).
- By religion, Jewish (18.52%) and Muslim (16.67%) students were among the most likely to pay for ChatGPT, while Catholics had the lowest rate (3.70%).

### Paid Subscription to Other Generative AI Applications

- Only 2.25% of students had a paid subscription to a generative AI application other than ChatGPT.
- Higher tuition students ($12,000–$20,000) were more likely to subscribe (4.20%) compared to those at lower tuition schools.
- Small college students (<5,000 enrollment) had the lowest paid subscription rates (1.59%), while mid-sized institutions had higher adoption.
- Older students (28+) had the highest subscription rate (4.64%).
- Students from abroad (5.49%) were more likely to pay for other generative AI applications than those from the U.S.
- Students in high-income families ($250,000+) had the highest subscription rates (3.33%), while those from lower-income families had similar rates.
- Very right-wing students were more likely to have a paid AI subscription (10.00%) compared to liberals (0.81%).
- STEM students, especially in Biology, Pre-Med, and Computer Science, had higher paid AI subscriptions (~3-4%).
- Males (3.22%) were more likely than females (1.77%) to pay for other generative AI applications.
- Students from Protestant backgrounds (2.00–13.04%) had more variance in subscription rates, with Evangelicals subscribing the most.
- Asian students (5.06%) had the highest paid subscription rates, while Black students had one of the lowest (1.50%).

### Use of Generative AI as a Substitute for or Complement to Internet Searches

- On average, students replaced or supplemented their usual search engine with generative AI applications 25.17% of the time. Note that this is a much higher rate than what we have found with other populations, such as lawyers or college professors, whose rates in this area hover around 10-15%.
- Higher tuition students ($12,000–$20,000) used generative AI as a complement or substitute for internet searches more often (28.56%) compared to lower tuition students (21.73%).

- Students at small and mid-sized colleges used AI more frequently (~26%) compared to large college students (22.16%).
- Older students (22-27) used AI search the most (27.59%), while students over 28 used it the least (21.60%).
- Urban students used AI searches more (27.21%) than rural students (23.15%).
- International students were the highest users of AI search (38.18%).
- First-year students used AI search more (26.32%) than seniors (25.93%) or sophomores (22.63%).
- Higher-income students ($250,000+) used AI searches the most (32.98%), while lower-income students ($50,000–$90,000) used it less (24.22%).
- Very right-wing students used AI searches much more often (41.54%) than very left-wing students (16.09%).
- Biology, Pre-Med (32.20%) and Nursing (30.64%) majors used AI searches the most, while Education (15.64%) and Fine Arts (17.11%) used it the least.
- Male students (26.60%) used AI search slightly more than females (25.61%), while transgender students used it the least (13.74%).
- Students living at home with parents used AI search more often (27.11%) than those in dorms (23.44%).
- Jobless students (28.63%) used AI search more than those with full-time jobs (19.36%).
- Asian (31.49%) and Latino (31.34%) students used AI search the most, while White students used it the least (22.76%).
- Jewish (37.50%) and Muslim (36.06%) students used AI search more than Christian groups.
- STEM students, especially in Computer Science and Biology, used AI searches frequently, while Humanities and Fine Arts students used it the least.

## Conclusions

1. Most students do not pay for ChatGPT or other generative AI tools. Adoption is higher among students at high-tuition colleges, private institutions, and STEM majors.
2. Generative AI usage varies significantly by demographic factors, with older, wealthier, and international students showing greater engagement.
3. Students from right-wing political backgrounds and high-income families were more likely to use and pay for AI services.
4. Generative AI is supplementing or replacing traditional search engines for about 25% of students' searches, with variations by major, region, and academic standing.
5. AI adoption is increasing in STEM and business fields, while Humanities and Arts students show more resistance.
6. Ethnicity, gender, and religious background play a role in AI adoption, with Asian and Jewish students among the highest users.

## Table 1 Which of the following have you used in the past month? (check all that apply)

### Table 1.1.1 Which of the following have you used in the past month? Microsoft CoPilot.

| | No Answer | Yes | No |
|---|---|---|---|
| Entire sample | 0.00% | 15.46% | 84.54% |

### Table 1.1.2 Which of the following have you used in the past month? Microsoft CoPilot. Broken out by tuition of college attended

| Tuition of college attended | Yes | No |
|---|---|---|
| Less than $6,000 | 12.73% | 87.27% |
| $6,000+ - $12,000 | 17.89% | 82.11% |
| $12,000+ - $20,000 | 20.23% | 79.77% |
| More than $20,000 | 10.93% | 89.07% |

### Table 1.1.3 Which of the following have you used in the past month? Microsoft CoPilot. Broken out by enrollment of college attended

| Enrollment of college attended | Yes | No |
|---|---|---|
| Less than 5,000 | 9.52% | 90.48% |
| 5,000+ - 12,000 | 19.62% | 80.38% |
| 12,000+ - 22,900 | 18.38% | 81.62% |
| More than 22,900 | 14.49% | 85.51% |

### Table 1.1.4 Which of the following have you used in the past month? Microsoft CoPilot. Broken out by public or private college

| Public or private college | Yes | No |
|---|---|---|
| Public | 16.88% | 83.12% |
| Private | 10.68% | 89.32% |

**Table 1.1.5 Which of the following have you used in the past month? Microsoft CoPilot. Broken out by age of respondent**

| Age of respondent | Yes | No |
|---|---|---|
| Under 19 | 12.93% | 87.07% |
| 19-21 | 13.45% | 86.55% |
| 22-27 | 18.48% | 81.52% |
| Over 28 | 19.59% | 80.41% |

**Table 1.1.6 Which of the following have you used in the past month? Microsoft CoPilot. Broken out by urban, suburban or rural upbringing**

| Urban, suburban or rural upbringing | Yes | No |
|---|---|---|
| I grew up in a major city with more than 350,000 people | 18.18% | 81.82% |
| I grew up in a small or medium sized city with less than 350,000 people. | 15.75% | 84.25% |
| I grew up in a suburban area | 14.15% | 85.85% |
| I grew up in a rural area. | 13.89% | 86.11% |
| Unknown | 0.00% | 100.00% |

**Table 1.1.7 Which of the following have you used in the past month? Microsoft CoPilot. Broken out by region of upbringing**

| Region of upbringing | Yes | No |
|---|---|---|
| The South | 14.29% | 85.71% |
| The Northeast | 11.11% | 88.89% |
| The Midwest | 15.33% | 84.67% |
| The West | 7.63% | 92.37% |
| Abroad | 25.61% | 74.39% |
| Unknown | 14.29% | 85.71% |

### Table 1.1.8 Which of the following have you used in the past month? Microsoft CoPilot. Broken out by year of class standing

| Year of class standing | Yes | No |
|---|---|---|
| First year student | 14.36% | 85.64% |
| Sophomore | 15.56% | 84.44% |
| Junior | 14.04% | 85.96% |
| Senior | 17.05% | 82.95% |
| Unknown | 31.25% | 68.75% |

### Table 1.1.9 Which of the following have you used in the past month? Microsoft CoPilot. Broken out by annual family of origin income level

| Annual family of origin income level | Yes | No |
|---|---|---|
| Less than $50,000 per year | 20.38% | 79.62% |
| $50,000 to $90,000 per year | 14.97% | 85.03% |
| $90,000+ to $150,000 per year | 11.11% | 88.89% |
| $150,000+ to $250,000 per year | 15.38% | 84.62% |
| More than $250,000 per year | 10.00% | 90.00% |
| Unknown | 13.64% | 86.36% |

**Table 1.1.10 Which of the following have you used in the past month? Microsoft CoPilot. Broken out by relationship with organized religion**

| Relationship with organized religion | Yes | No |
|---|---|---|
| I practice a religion thoroughly and consider my religion to be a very important part of my life. | 20.41% | 79.59% |
| I practice a religion and try to attend regular services and to participate as much as I can. | 20.38% | 79.62% |
| I identify with a religion but can't say I put a lot of effort into practicing it. | 15.33% | 84.67% |
| I don't really believe in or practice an organized religion. | 11.11% | 88.89% |
| Unknown | 12.50% | 87.50% |

**Table 1.1.11 Which of the following have you used in the past month? Microsoft CoPilot. Broken out by political views**

| Political views | Yes | No |
|---|---|---|
| Very left wing | 13.25% | 86.75% |
| Liberal | 10.57% | 89.43% |
| Middle of the road | 19.70% | 80.30% |
| Conservative | 19.57% | 80.43% |
| Very right wing | 15.00% | 85.00% |
| Unknown | 33.33% | 66.67% |

**Table 1.1.12 Which of the following have you used in the past month? Microsoft CoPilot. Broken out by college grades**

| College grades | Yes | No |
|---|---|---|
| A or A- average or more | 15.73% | 84.27% |
| B or B+ average | 14.95% | 85.05% |
| C or C+ or lower | 16.13% | 83.87% |
| Unknown | 0.00% | 100.00% |

**Table 1.1.13 Which of the following have you used in the past month? Microsoft CoPilot. Broken out by academic major**

| Academic major | Yes | No |
|---|---|---|
| Business, Economics or Finance | 19.05% | 80.95% |
| Psychology | 18.09% | 81.91% |
| Education or Library Science | 13.51% | 86.49% |
| Criminology/Law Enforcement | 26.67% | 73.33% |
| Occupational or Physical Therapy, Nursing, Public Health, Nutrition. other Health-Related | 12.96% | 87.04% |
| Communications, Media, Journalism | 8.33% | 91.67% |
| Fine Arts and Architecture | 4.76% | 95.24% |
| Music, Dance, Theater, other Performing Arts | 15.38% | 84.62% |
| English, Foreign Languages, Comp Literature, Creative Writing | 0.00% | 100.00% |
| Biology, Physics, Chemistry, Pre-Med | 13.53% | 86.47% |
| Geology, Oceanography, Environmental Sciences | 3.85% | 96.15% |
| Engineering, Mathematics, Computer Science | 26.24% | 73.76% |
| History, Classics | 7.69% | 92.31% |
| Sociology, Political Science, Anthropology or other Social Science, except Economics and Psychology | 6.58% | 93.42% |
| Other | 15.38% | 84.62% |

**Table 1.1.14 Which of the following have you used in the past month? Microsoft CoPilot. Broken out by gender of respondent**

| Gender of respondent | Yes | No |
|---|---|---|
| Male | 22.81% | 77.19% |
| Female | 12.42% | 87.58% |
| Transgender | 5.26% | 94.74% |
| Unknown | 0.00% | 100.00% |

### Table 1.1.15 Which of the following have you used in the past month? Microsoft CoPilot. Broken out by status of current residency

| Status of current residency | Yes | No |
|---|---|---|
| At home with my parents or guardian | 12.67% | 87.33% |
| Off campus with others who are not my parents or guardian | 17.46% | 82.54% |
| Off campus alone | 21.74% | 78.26% |
| On campus in the dorms or college-provided suites | 14.15% | 85.85% |
| Unknown | 0.00% | 100.00% |

### Table 1.1.16 Which of the following have you used in the past month? Microsoft CoPilot. Broken out by current employment situation

| Current employment situation | Yes | No |
|---|---|---|
| I don't have a full or part time job. | 16.43% | 83.57% |
| I have a part time job. | 13.56% | 86.44% |
| I have a full time job. | 19.08% | 80.92% |
| Unknown | 0.00% | 100.00% |

### Table 1.1.17 Which of the following have you used in the past month? Microsoft CoPilot. Broken out by sexual orientation

| Sexual orientation | Yes | No |
|---|---|---|
| Heterosexual or "straight" | 17.25% | 82.75% |
| Homosexual or "gay" | 13.51% | 86.49% |
| Bi-sexual | 9.35% | 90.65% |
| Unknown | 26.67% | 73.33% |

**Table 1.1.18 Which of the following have you used in the past month? Microsoft CoPilot. Broken out by SAT or ACT score**

| SAT or ACT score | Yes | No |
|---|---|---|
| 30 or over ACT or 1350 or over SAT | 13.55% | 86.45% |
| 24-29 ACT or 1170 to 1349 SAT | 13.23% | 86.77% |
| 20-23 ACT or 1050 to 1169 SAT | 10.56% | 89.44% |
| 17-19 ACT or 900 to 1050 SAT | 18.18% | 81.82% |
| 16 or Under ACT or Under 900 SAT | 11.11% | 88.89% |
| Never took either test | 24.04% | 75.96% |
| Unknown | 18.18% | 81.82% |

**Table 1.1.19 Which of the following have you used in the past month? Microsoft CoPilot. Broken out by race or ethnicity**

| Race or ethnicity | Yes | No |
|---|---|---|
| White or Caucasian | 12.33% | 87.67% |
| Black or African American | 21.80% | 78.20% |
| Latino or Hispanic | 12.50% | 87.50% |
| Asian or Asian American | 22.47% | 77.53% |
| American Indigenous, Eskimo, Pacific Islander, Hawaiian Native | 0.00% | 100.00% |
| Mixed race | 14.08% | 85.92% |
| Unknown | 16.67% | 83.33% |

**Table 1.1.20 Which of the following have you used in the past month? Microsoft CoPilot. Broken out by religion**

| Religion | Yes | No |
|---|---|---|
| I do not practice or identify with an organized religion | 10.76% | 89.24% |
| Hinduism | 36.00% | 64.00% |
| Islam | 16.67% | 83.33% |
| Judaism | 3.70% | 96.30% |
| Mormon | 16.67% | 83.33% |
| Catholic | 18.52% | 81.48% |
| Lutheran | 9.38% | 90.63% |
| Baptist | 23.81% | 76.19% |
| Evangelical Protestant Christianity | 8.70% | 91.30% |
| Protestant Christianity | 14.00% | 86.00% |
| Orthodox Christianity | 5.56% | 94.44% |
| Buddhism | 25.00% | 75.00% |
| Non-Denominational Christianity | 15.32% | 84.68% |
| Other | 24.14% | 75.86% |

**Table 1.2.1 Which of the following have you used in the past month? ChatGPT (any version).**

| | No Answer | Yes | No |
|---|---|---|---|
| Entire sample | 0.00% | 64.77% | 35.23% |

**Table 1.2.2 Which of the following have you used in the past month? ChatGPT (any version). Broken out by tuition of college attended**

| Tuition of college attended | Yes | No |
|---|---|---|
| Less than $6,000 | 53.93% | 46.07% |
| $6,000+ - $12,000 | 61.79% | 38.21% |
| $12,000+ - $20,000 | 64.89% | 35.11% |
| More than $20,000 | 79.35% | 20.65% |

**Table 1.2.3 Which of the following have you used in the past month? ChatGPT (any version). Broken out by enrollment of college attended**

| Enrollment of college attended | Yes | No |
|---|---|---|
| Less than 5,000 | 76.19% | 23.81% |
| 5,000+ - 12,000 | 65.38% | 34.62% |
| 12,000+ - 22,900 | 62.82% | 37.18% |
| More than 22,900 | 55.43% | 44.57% |

**Table 1.2.4 Which of the following have you used in the past month? ChatGPT (any version). Broken out by public or private college**

| Public or private college | Yes | No |
|---|---|---|
| Public | 61.04% | 38.96% |
| Private | 77.35% | 22.65% |

**Table 1.2.5 Which of the following have you used in the past month? ChatGPT (any version). Broken out by age of respondent**

| Age of respondent | Yes | No |
|---|---|---|
| Under 19 | 63.59% | 36.41% |
| 19-21 | 67.65% | 32.35% |
| 22-27 | 65.88% | 34.12% |
| Over 28 | 62.37% | 37.63% |

**Table 1.2.6 Which of the following have you used in the past month? ChatGPT (any version). Broken out by urban, suburban or rural upbringing**

| Urban, suburban or rural upbringing | Yes | No |
|---|---|---|
| I grew up in a major city with more than 350,000 people | 70.08% | 29.92% |
| I grew up in a small or medium sized city with less than 350,000 people. | 69.29% | 30.71% |
| I grew up in a suburban area | 61.64% | 38.36% |
| I grew up in a rural area. | 57.22% | 42.78% |
| Unknown | 33.33% | 66.67% |

**Table 1.2.7 Which of the following have you used in the past month? ChatGPT (any version). Broken out by region of upbringing**

| Region of upbringing | Yes | No |
|---|---|---|
| The South | 61.22% | 38.78% |
| The Northeast | 62.22% | 37.78% |
| The Midwest | 58.04% | 41.96% |
| The West | 76.27% | 23.73% |
| Abroad | 81.10% | 18.90% |
| Unknown | 28.57% | 71.43% |

**Table 1.2.8 Which of the following have you used in the past month? ChatGPT (any version). Broken out by year of class standing**

| Year of class standing | Yes | No |
|---|---|---|
| First year student | 64.48% | 35.52% |
| Sophomore | 63.89% | 36.11% |
| Junior | 59.65% | 40.35% |
| Senior | 69.77% | 30.23% |
| Unknown | 56.25% | 43.75% |

**Table 1.2.9 Which of the following have you used in the past month? ChatGPT (any version). Broken out by annual family of origin income level**

| Annual family of origin income level | Yes | No |
|---|---|---|
| Less than $50,000 per year | 65.92% | 34.08% |
| $50,000 to $90,000 per year | 60.54% | 39.46% |
| $90,000+ to $150,000 per year | 65.66% | 34.34% |
| $150,000+ to $250,000 per year | 71.15% | 28.85% |
| More than $250,000 per year | 66.67% | 33.33% |
| Unknown | 59.09% | 40.91% |

**Table 1.2.10 Which of the following have you used in the past month? ChatGPT (any version). Broken out by relationship with organized religion**

| Relationship with organized religion | Yes | No |
|---|---|---|
| I practice a religion thoroughly and consider my religion to be a very important part of my life. | 63.78% | 36.22% |
| I practice a religion and try to attend regular services and to participate as much as I can. | 66.24% | 33.76% |
| I identify with a religion but can't say I put a lot of effort into practicing it. | 64.96% | 35.04% |
| I don't really believe in or practice an organized religion. | 64.86% | 35.14% |
| Unknown | 50.00% | 50.00% |

**Table 1.2.11 Which of the following have you used in the past month? ChatGPT (any version). Broken out by political views**

| Political views | Yes | No |
|---|---|---|
| Very left wing | 52.32% | 47.68% |
| Liberal | 68.29% | 31.71% |
| Middle of the road | 69.25% | 30.75% |
| Conservative | 60.87% | 39.13% |
| Very right wing | 55.00% | 45.00% |
| Unknown | 44.44% | 55.56% |

**Table 1.2.12 Which of the following have you used in the past month? ChatGPT (any version). Broken out by college grades**

| College grades | Yes | No |
|---|---|---|
| A or A- average or more | 67.18% | 32.82% |
| B or B+ average | 63.46% | 36.54% |
| C or C+ or lower | 50.00% | 50.00% |
| Unknown | 0.00% | 100.00% |

**Table 1.2.13 Which of the following have you used in the past month? ChatGPT (any version). Broken out by academic major**

| Academic major | Yes | No |
|---|---|---|
| Business, Economics or Finance | 73.02% | 26.98% |
| Psychology | 59.57% | 40.43% |
| Education or Library Science | 60.81% | 39.19% |
| Criminology/Law Enforcement | 40.00% | 60.00% |
| Occupational or Physical Therapy, Nursing, Public Health, Nutrition. other Health-Related | 62.96% | 37.04% |
| Communications, Media, Journalism | 70.83% | 29.17% |
| Fine Arts and Architecture | 53.97% | 46.03% |
| Music, Dance, Theater, other Performing Arts | 53.85% | 46.15% |
| English, Foreign Languages, Comp Literature, Creative Writing | 48.28% | 51.72% |
| Biology, Physics, Chemistry, Pre-Med | 65.41% | 34.59% |
| Geology, Oceanography, Environmental Sciences | 46.15% | 53.85% |
| Engineering, Mathematics, Computer Science | 77.72% | 22.28% |
| History, Classics | 46.15% | 53.85% |
| Sociology, Political Science, Anthropology or other Social Science, except Economics and Psychology | 64.47% | 35.53% |
| Other | 38.46% | 61.54% |

**Table 1.2.14 Which of the following have you used in the past month? ChatGPT (any version). Broken out by gender of respondent**

| Gender of respondent | Yes | No |
|---|---|---|
| Male | 73.98% | 26.02% |
| Female | 61.61% | 38.39% |
| Transgender | 45.61% | 54.39% |
| Unknown | 33.33% | 66.67% |

**Table 1.2.15 Which of the following have you used in the past month? ChatGPT (any version). Broken out by status of current residency**

| Status of current residency | Yes | No |
|---|---|---|
| At home with my parents or guardian | 59.73% | 40.27% |
| Off campus with others who are not my parents or guardian | 66.27% | 33.73% |
| Off campus alone | 63.48% | 36.52% |
| On campus in the dorms or college-provided suites | 67.05% | 32.95% |
| Unknown | 33.33% | 66.67% |

**Table 1.2.16 Which of the following have you used in the past month? ChatGPT (any version). Broken out by current employment situation**

| Current employment situation | Yes | No |
|---|---|---|
| I don't have a full or part time job. | 66.43% | 33.57% |
| I have a part time job. | 67.11% | 32.89% |
| I have a full time job. | 54.61% | 45.39% |
| Unknown | 33.33% | 66.67% |

**Table 1.2.17 Which of the following have you used in the past month? ChatGPT (any version). Broken out by sexual orientation**

| Sexual orientation | Yes | No |
|---|---|---|
| Heterosexual or "straight" | 68.29% | 31.71% |
| Homosexual or "gay" | 63.51% | 36.49% |
| Bi-sexual | 55.61% | 44.39% |
| Unknown | 33.33% | 66.67% |

### Table 1.2.18 Which of the following have you used in the past month? ChatGPT (any version). Broken out by SAT or ACT score

| SAT or ACT score | Yes | No |
|---|---|---|
| 30 or over ACT or 1350 or over SAT | 69.32% | 30.68% |
| 24-29 ACT or 1170 to 1349 SAT | 64.98% | 35.02% |
| 20-23 ACT or 1050 to 1169 SAT | 57.22% | 42.78% |
| 17-19 ACT or 900 to 1050 SAT | 54.55% | 45.45% |
| 16 or Under ACT or Under 900 SAT | 66.67% | 33.33% |
| Never took either test | 70.19% | 29.81% |
| Unknown | 54.55% | 45.45% |

### Table 1.2.19 Which of the following have you used in the past month? ChatGPT (any version). Broken out by race or ethnicity

| Race or ethnicity | Yes | No |
|---|---|---|
| White or Caucasian | 60.31% | 39.69% |
| Black or African American | 63.91% | 36.09% |
| Latino or Hispanic | 63.46% | 36.54% |
| Asian or Asian American | 78.65% | 21.35% |
| American Indigenous, Eskimo, Pacific Islander, Hawaiian Native | 40.00% | 60.00% |
| Mixed race | 69.01% | 30.99% |
| Unknown | 58.33% | 41.67% |

**Table 1.2.20 Which of the following have you used in the past month? ChatGPT (any version). Broken out by religion**

| Religion | Yes | No |
|---|---|---|
| I do not practice or identify with an organized religion | 64.83% | 35.17% |
| Hinduism | 72.00% | 28.00% |
| Islam | 64.58% | 35.42% |
| Judaism | 66.67% | 33.33% |
| Mormon | 66.67% | 33.33% |
| Catholic | 70.37% | 29.63% |
| Lutheran | 62.50% | 37.50% |
| Baptist | 49.21% | 50.79% |
| Evangelical Protestant Christianity | 69.57% | 30.43% |
| Protestant Christianity | 64.00% | 36.00% |
| Orthodox Christianity | 72.22% | 27.78% |
| Buddhism | 80.00% | 20.00% |
| Non-Denominational Christianity | 59.46% | 40.54% |
| Other | 63.79% | 36.21% |

**Table 1.3.1 Which of the following have you used in the past month? Gemini.**

| | No Answer | Yes | No |
|---|---|---|---|
| Entire sample | 0.00% | 13.60% | 86.40% |

**Table 1.3.2 Which of the following have you used in the past month? Gemini. Broken out by tuition of college attended**

| Tuition of college attended | Yes | No |
|---|---|---|
| Less than $6,000 | 12.36% | 87.64% |
| $6,000+ - $12,000 | 15.04% | 84.96% |
| $12,000+ - $20,000 | 14.50% | 85.50% |
| More than $20,000 | 12.55% | 87.45% |

**Table 1.3.3 Which of the following have you used in the past month? Gemini. Broken out by enrollment of college attended**

| Enrollment of college attended | Yes | No |
|---|---|---|
| Less than 5,000 | 11.11% | 88.89% |
| 5,000+ - 12,000 | 14.23% | 85.77% |
| 12,000+ - 22,900 | 16.67% | 83.33% |
| More than 22,900 | 12.68% | 87.32% |

**Table 1.3.4 Which of the following have you used in the past month? Gemini. Broken out by public or private college**

| Public or private college | Yes | No |
|---|---|---|
| Public | 13.83% | 86.17% |
| Private | 12.82% | 87.18% |

**Table 1.3.5 Which of the following have you used in the past month? Gemini. Broken out by age of respondent**

| Age of respondent | Yes | No |
|---|---|---|
| Under 19 | 12.14% | 87.86% |
| 19-21 | 15.97% | 84.03% |
| 22-27 | 12.32% | 87.68% |
| Over 28 | 14.95% | 85.05% |

**Table 1.3.6 Which of the following have you used in the past month? Gemini. Broken out by urban, suburban or rural upbringing**

| Urban, suburban or rural upbringing | Yes | No |
|---|---|---|
| I grew up in a major city with more than 350,000 people | 16.29% | 83.71% |
| I grew up in a small or medium sized city with less than 350,000 people. | 13.39% | 86.61% |
| I grew up in a suburban area | 12.89% | 87.11% |
| I grew up in a rural area. | 11.11% | 88.89% |
| Unknown | 16.67% | 83.33% |

**Table 1.3.7 Which of the following have you used in the past month? Gemini. Broken out by region of upbringing**

| Region of upbringing | Yes | No |
|---|---|---|
| The South | 11.43% | 88.57% |
| The Northeast | 10.00% | 90.00% |
| The Midwest | 11.81% | 88.19% |
| The West | 11.02% | 88.98% |
| Abroad | 25.61% | 74.39% |
| Unknown | 0.00% | 100.00% |

**Table 1.3.8 Which of the following have you used in the past month? Gemini. Broken out by year of class standing**

| Year of class standing | Yes | No |
|---|---|---|
| First year student | 13.85% | 86.15% |
| Sophomore | 11.67% | 88.33% |
| Junior | 11.70% | 88.30% |
| Senior | 15.50% | 84.50% |
| Unknown | 18.75% | 81.25% |

**Table 1.3.9 Which of the following have you used in the past month? Gemini. Broken out by annual family of origin income level**

| Annual family of origin income level | Yes | No |
|---|---|---|
| Less than $50,000 per year | 17.20% | 82.80% |
| $50,000 to $90,000 per year | 11.56% | 88.44% |
| $90,000+ to $150,000 per year | 10.61% | 89.39% |
| $150,000+ to $250,000 per year | 16.35% | 83.65% |
| More than $250,000 per year | 11.11% | 88.89% |
| Unknown | 13.64% | 86.36% |

**Table 1.3.10 Which of the following have you used in the past month? Gemini. Broken out by relationship with organized religion**

| Relationship with organized religion | Yes | No |
|---|---|---|
| I practice a religion thoroughly and consider my religion to be a very important part of my life. | 16.33% | 83.67% |
| I practice a religion and try to attend regular services and to participate as much as I can. | 12.10% | 87.90% |
| I identify with a religion but can't say I put a lot of effort into practicing it. | 14.60% | 85.40% |
| I don't really believe in or practice an organized religion. | 11.63% | 88.37% |
| Unknown | 37.50% | 62.50% |

**Table 1.3.11 Which of the following have you used in the past month? Gemini. Broken out by political views**

| Political views | Yes | No |
|---|---|---|
| Very left wing | 9.93% | 90.07% |
| Liberal | 15.72% | 84.28% |
| Middle of the road | 13.43% | 86.57% |
| Conservative | 13.04% | 86.96% |
| Very right wing | 10.00% | 90.00% |
| Unknown | 11.11% | 88.89% |

**Table 1.3.12 Which of the following have you used in the past month? Gemini. Broken out by college grades**

| College grades | Yes | No |
|---|---|---|
| A or A- average or more | 13.28% | 86.72% |
| B or B+ average | 14.95% | 85.05% |
| C or C+ or lower | 11.29% | 88.71% |
| Unknown | 0.00% | 100.00% |

### Table 1.3.13 Which of the following have you used in the past month? Gemini. Broken out by academic major

| Academic major | Yes | No |
|---|---|---|
| Business, Economics or Finance | 15.87% | 84.13% |
| Psychology | 9.57% | 90.43% |
| Education or Library Science | 10.81% | 89.19% |
| Criminology/Law Enforcement | 6.67% | 93.33% |
| Occupational or Physical Therapy, Nursing, Public Health, Nutrition. other Health-Related | 11.11% | 88.89% |
| Communications, Media, Journalism | 12.50% | 87.50% |
| Fine Arts and Architecture | 6.35% | 93.65% |
| Music, Dance, Theater, other Performing Arts | 0.00% | 100.00% |
| English, Foreign Languages, Comp Literature, Creative Writing | 10.34% | 89.66% |
| Biology, Physics, Chemistry, Pre-Med | 13.53% | 86.47% |
| Geology, Oceanography, Environmental Sciences | 11.54% | 88.46% |
| Engineering, Mathematics, Computer Science | 22.77% | 77.23% |
| History, Classics | 15.38% | 84.62% |
| Sociology, Political Science, Anthropology or other Social Science, except Economics and Psychology | 11.84% | 88.16% |
| Other | 7.69% | 92.31% |

### Table 1.3.14 Which of the following have you used in the past month? Gemini. Broken out by gender of respondent

| Gender of respondent | Yes | No |
|---|---|---|
| Male | 19.59% | 80.41% |
| Female | 10.32% | 89.68% |
| Transgender | 14.04% | 85.96% |
| Unknown | 0.00% | 100.00% |

**Table 1.3.15 Which of the following have you used in the past month? Gemini. Broken out by status of current residency**

| Status of current residency | Yes | No |
|---|---|---|
| At home with my parents or guardian | 10.41% | 89.59% |
| Off campus with others who are not my parents or guardian | 15.48% | 84.52% |
| Off campus alone | 20.00% | 80.00% |
| On campus in the dorms or college-provided suites | 12.53% | 87.47% |
| Unknown | 0.00% | 100.00% |

**Table 1.3.16 Which of the following have you used in the past month? Gemini. Broken out by current employment situation**

| Current employment situation | Yes | No |
|---|---|---|
| I don't have a full or part time job. | 13.53% | 86.47% |
| I have a part time job. | 13.56% | 86.44% |
| I have a full time job. | 14.47% | 85.53% |
| Unknown | 0.00% | 100.00% |

**Table 1.3.17 Which of the following have you used in the past month? Gemini. Broken out by sexual orientation**

| Sexual orientation | Yes | No |
|---|---|---|
| Heterosexual or "straight" | 15.16% | 84.84% |
| Homosexual or "gay" | 2.70% | 97.30% |
| Bi-sexual | 12.15% | 87.85% |
| Unknown | 13.33% | 86.67% |

**Table 1.3.18 Which of the following have you used in the past month? Gemini. Broken out by SAT or ACT score**

| SAT or ACT score | Yes | No |
|---|---|---|
| 30 or over ACT or 1350 or over SAT | 13.55% | 86.45% |
| 24-29 ACT or 1170 to 1349 SAT | 13.62% | 86.38% |
| 20-23 ACT or 1050 to 1169 SAT | 9.44% | 90.56% |
| 17-19 ACT or 900 to 1050 SAT | 9.09% | 90.91% |
| 16 or Under ACT or Under 900 SAT | 11.11% | 88.89% |
| Never took either test | 19.23% | 80.77% |
| Unknown | 18.18% | 81.82% |

**Table 1.3.19 Which of the following have you used in the past month? Gemini. Broken out by race or ethnicity**

| Race or ethnicity | Yes | No |
|---|---|---|
| White or Caucasian | 11.18% | 88.82% |
| Black or African American | 19.55% | 80.45% |
| Latino or Hispanic | 8.65% | 91.35% |
| Asian or Asian American | 19.10% | 80.90% |
| American Indigenous, Eskimo, Pacific Islander, Hawaiian Native | 0.00% | 100.00% |
| Mixed race | 12.68% | 87.32% |
| Unknown | 25.00% | 75.00% |

**Table 1.3.20 Which of the following have you used in the past month? Gemini. Broken out by religion**

| Religion | Yes | No |
|---|---|---|
| I do not practice or identify with an organized religion | 10.50% | 89.50% |
| Hinduism | 34.00% | 66.00% |
| Islam | 18.75% | 81.25% |
| Judaism | 7.41% | 92.59% |
| Mormon | 16.67% | 83.33% |
| Catholic | 11.11% | 88.89% |
| Lutheran | 21.88% | 78.13% |
| Baptist | 11.11% | 88.89% |
| Evangelical Protestant Christianity | 17.39% | 82.61% |
| Protestant Christianity | 12.00% | 88.00% |
| Orthodox Christianity | 11.11% | 88.89% |
| Buddhism | 20.00% | 80.00% |
| Non-Denominational Christianity | 12.61% | 87.39% |
| Other | 18.97% | 81.03% |

**Table 1.4.1 Which of the following have you used in the past month? Claude.**

| | No Answer | Yes | No |
|---|---|---|---|
| Entire sample | 0.00% | 5.77% | 94.23% |

**Table 1.4.2 Which of the following have you used in the past month? Claude. Broken out by tuition of college attended**

| Tuition of college attended | Yes | No |
|---|---|---|
| Less than $6,000 | 3.00% | 97.00% |
| $6,000+ - $12,000 | 4.07% | 95.93% |
| $12,000+ - $20,000 | 6.11% | 93.89% |
| More than $20,000 | 10.12% | 89.88% |

**Table 1.4.3 Which of the following have you used in the past month? Claude. Broken out by enrollment of college attended**

| Enrollment of college attended | Yes | No |
|---|---|---|
| Less than 5,000 | 9.13% | 90.87% |
| 5,000+ - 12,000 | 3.46% | 96.54% |
| 12,000+ - 22,900 | 7.69% | 92.31% |
| More than 22,900 | 3.26% | 96.74% |

**Table 1.4.4 Which of the following have you used in the past month? Claude. Broken out by public or private college**

| Public or private college | Yes | No |
|---|---|---|
| Public | 4.31% | 95.69% |
| Private | 10.68% | 89.32% |

**Table 1.4.5 Which of the following have you used in the past month? Claude. Broken out by age of respondent**

| Age of respondent | Yes | No |
|---|---|---|
| Under 19 | 4.22% | 95.78% |
| 19-21 | 5.04% | 94.96% |
| 22-27 | 7.58% | 92.42% |
| Over 28 | 7.73% | 92.27% |

**Table 1.4.6 Which of the following have you used in the past month? Claude. Broken out by urban, suburban or rural upbringing**

| Urban, suburban or rural upbringing | Yes | No |
|---|---|---|
| I grew up in a major city with more than 350,000 people | 9.47% | 90.53% |
| I grew up in a small or medium sized city with less than 350,000 people. | 4.72% | 95.28% |
| I grew up in a suburban area | 5.35% | 94.65% |
| I grew up in a rural area. | 2.78% | 97.22% |
| Unknown | 0.00% | 100.00% |

### Table 1.4.7 Which of the following have you used in the past month? Claude. Broken out by region of upbringing

| Region of upbringing | Yes | No |
|---|---|---|
| The South | 4.90% | 95.10% |
| The Northeast | 4.44% | 95.56% |
| The Midwest | 2.51% | 97.49% |
| The West | 9.32% | 90.68% |
| Abroad | 13.41% | 86.59% |
| Unknown | 0.00% | 100.00% |

### Table 1.4.8 Which of the following have you used in the past month? Claude. Broken out by year of class standing

| Year of class standing | Yes | No |
|---|---|---|
| First year student | 5.29% | 94.71% |
| Sophomore | 5.56% | 94.44% |
| Junior | 4.68% | 95.32% |
| Senior | 7.36% | 92.64% |
| Unknown | 6.25% | 93.75% |

### Table 1.4.9 Which of the following have you used in the past month? Claude. Broken out by annual family of origin income level

| Annual family of origin income level | Yes | No |
|---|---|---|
| Less than $50,000 per year | 5.73% | 94.27% |
| $50,000 to $90,000 per year | 4.42% | 95.58% |
| $90,000+ to $150,000 per year | 4.04% | 95.96% |
| $150,000+ to $250,000 per year | 10.58% | 89.42% |
| More than $250,000 per year | 8.89% | 91.11% |
| Unknown | 4.55% | 95.45% |

**Table 1.4.10 Which of the following have you used in the past month? Claude. Broken out by relationship with organized religion**

| Relationship with organized religion | Yes | No |
|---|---|---|
| I practice a religion thoroughly and consider my religion to be a very important part of my life. | 5.61% | 94.39% |
| I practice a religion and try to attend regular services and to participate as much as I can. | 4.46% | 95.54% |
| I identify with a religion but can't say I put a lot of effort into practicing it. | 6.20% | 93.80% |
| I don't really believe in or practice an organized religion. | 6.20% | 93.80% |
| Unknown | 0.00% | 100.00% |

**Table 1.4.11 Which of the following have you used in the past month? Claude. Broken out by political views**

| Political views | Yes | No |
|---|---|---|
| Very left wing | 3.97% | 96.03% |
| Liberal | 6.23% | 93.77% |
| Middle of the road | 6.87% | 93.13% |
| Conservative | 2.90% | 97.10% |
| Very right wing | 15.00% | 85.00% |
| Unknown | 0.00% | 100.00% |

**Table 1.4.12 Which of the following have you used in the past month? Claude. Broken out by college grades**

| College grades | Yes | No |
|---|---|---|
| A or A- average or more | 7.48% | 92.52% |
| B or B+ average | 3.32% | 96.68% |
| C or C+ or lower | 0.00% | 100.00% |
| Unknown | 0.00% | 100.00% |

### Table 1.4.13 Which of the following have you used in the past month? Claude. Broken out by academic major

| Academic major | Yes | No |
|---|---|---|
| Business, Economics or Finance | 4.76% | 95.24% |
| Psychology | 4.26% | 95.74% |
| Education or Library Science | 4.05% | 95.95% |
| Criminology/Law Enforcement | 0.00% | 100.00% |
| Occupational or Physical Therapy, Nursing, Public Health, Nutrition. other Health-Related | 1.85% | 98.15% |
| Communications, Media, Journalism | 0.00% | 100.00% |
| Fine Arts and Architecture | 0.00% | 100.00% |
| Music, Dance, Theater, other Performing Arts | 0.00% | 100.00% |
| English, Foreign Languages, Comp Literature, Creative Writing | 0.00% | 100.00% |
| Biology, Physics, Chemistry, Pre-Med | 8.27% | 91.73% |
| Geology, Oceanography, Environmental Sciences | 0.00% | 100.00% |
| Engineering, Mathematics, Computer Science | 14.36% | 85.64% |
| History, Classics | 7.69% | 92.31% |
| Sociology, Political Science, Anthropology or other Social Science, except Economics and Psychology | 3.95% | 96.05% |
| Other | 0.00% | 100.00% |

### Table 1.4.14 Which of the following have you used in the past month? Claude. Broken out by gender of respondent

| Gender of respondent | Yes | No |
|---|---|---|
| Male | 8.77% | 91.23% |
| Female | 4.52% | 95.48% |
| Transgender | 1.75% | 98.25% |
| Unknown | 0.00% | 100.00% |

### Table 1.4.15 Which of the following have you used in the past month? Claude. Broken out by status of current residency

| Status of current residency | Yes | No |
|---|---|---|
| At home with my parents or guardian | 3.17% | 96.83% |
| Off campus with others who are not my parents or guardian | 4.76% | 95.24% |
| Off campus alone | 7.83% | 92.17% |
| On campus in the dorms or college-provided suites | 7.19% | 92.81% |
| Unknown | 0.00% | 100.00% |

### Table 1.4.16 Which of the following have you used in the past month? Claude. Broken out by current employment situation

| Current employment situation | Yes | No |
|---|---|---|
| I don't have a full or part time job. | 6.76% | 93.24% |
| I have a part time job. | 5.56% | 94.44% |
| I have a full time job. | 3.95% | 96.05% |
| Unknown | 0.00% | 100.00% |

### Table 1.4.17 Which of the following have you used in the past month? Claude. Broken out by sexual orientation

| Sexual orientation | Yes | No |
|---|---|---|
| Heterosexual or "straight" | 6.26% | 93.74% |
| Homosexual or "gay" | 8.11% | 91.89% |
| Bi-sexual | 2.80% | 97.20% |
| Unknown | 13.33% | 86.67% |

### Table 1.4.18 Which of the following have you used in the past month? Claude. Broken out by SAT or ACT score

| SAT or ACT score | Yes | No |
|---|---|---|
| 30 or over ACT or 1350 or over SAT | 11.16% | 88.84% |
| 24-29 ACT or 1170 to 1349 SAT | 3.50% | 96.50% |
| 20-23 ACT or 1050 to 1169 SAT | 1.67% | 98.33% |
| 17-19 ACT or 900 to 1050 SAT | 2.27% | 97.73% |
| 16 or Under ACT or Under 900 SAT | 3.70% | 96.30% |
| Never took either test | 7.69% | 92.31% |
| Unknown | 0.00% | 100.00% |

### Table 1.4.19 Which of the following have you used in the past month? Claude. Broken out by race or ethnicity

| Race or ethnicity | Yes | No |
|---|---|---|
| White or Caucasian | 4.43% | 95.57% |
| Black or African American | 5.26% | 94.74% |
| Latino or Hispanic | 2.88% | 97.12% |
| Asian or Asian American | 11.24% | 88.76% |
| American Indigenous, Eskimo, Pacific Islander, Hawaiian Native | 0.00% | 100.00% |
| Mixed race | 5.63% | 94.37% |
| Unknown | 16.67% | 83.33% |

### Table 1.4.20 Which of the following have you used in the past month? Claude. Broken out by religion

| Religion | Yes | No |
|---|---|---|
| I do not practice or identify with an organized religion | 6.30% | 93.70% |
| Hinduism | 10.00% | 90.00% |
| Islam | 10.42% | 89.58% |
| Judaism | 7.41% | 92.59% |
| Mormon | 0.00% | 100.00% |
| Catholic | 4.44% | 95.56% |
| Lutheran | 6.25% | 93.75% |
| Baptist | 1.59% | 98.41% |
| Evangelical Protestant Christianity | 13.04% | 86.96% |
| Protestant Christianity | 2.00% | 98.00% |
| Orthodox Christianity | 5.56% | 94.44% |
| Buddhism | 5.00% | 95.00% |
| Non-Denominational Christianity | 3.60% | 96.40% |
| Other | 6.90% | 93.10% |

### Table 1.5.1 Which of the following have you used in the past month? Midjourney.

| | No Answer | Yes | No |
|---|---|---|---|
| Entire sample | 0.00% | 1.66% | 98.34% |

### Table 1.5.2 Which of the following have you used in the past month? Midjourney. Broken out by tuition of college attended

| Tuition of college attended | Yes | No |
|---|---|---|
| Less than $6,000 | 1.50% | 98.50% |
| $6,000+ - $12,000 | 2.85% | 97.15% |
| $12,000+ - $20,000 | 1.15% | 98.85% |
| More than $20,000 | 1.21% | 98.79% |

**Table 1.5.3 Which of the following have you used in the past month? Midjourney. Broken out by enrollment of college attended**

| Enrollment of college attended | Yes | No |
|---|---|---|
| Less than 5,000 | 1.19% | 98.81% |
| 5,000+ - 12,000 | 1.92% | 98.08% |
| 12,000+ - 22,900 | 2.14% | 97.86% |
| More than 22,900 | 1.45% | 98.55% |

**Table 1.5.4 Which of the following have you used in the past month? Midjourney. Broken out by public or private college**

| Public or private college | Yes | No |
|---|---|---|
| Public | 1.78% | 98.22% |
| Private | 1.28% | 98.72% |

**Table 1.5.5 Which of the following have you used in the past month? Midjourney. Broken out by age of respondent**

| Age of respondent | Yes | No |
|---|---|---|
| Under 19 | 1.58% | 98.42% |
| 19-21 | 1.26% | 98.74% |
| 22-27 | 2.37% | 97.63% |
| Over 28 | 1.55% | 98.45% |

**Table 1.5.6 Which of the following have you used in the past month? Midjourney. Broken out by urban, suburban or rural upbringing**

| Urban, suburban or rural upbringing | Yes | No |
|---|---|---|
| I grew up in a major city with more than 350,000 people | 2.27% | 97.73% |
| I grew up in a small or medium sized city with less than 350,000 people. | 1.57% | 98.43% |
| I grew up in a suburban area | 1.26% | 98.74% |
| I grew up in a rural area. | 1.67% | 98.33% |
| Unknown | 0.00% | 100.00% |

**Table 1.5.7 Which of the following have you used in the past month? Midjourney. Broken out by region of upbringing**

| Region of upbringing | Yes | No |
|---|---|---|
| The South | 0.41% | 99.59% |
| The Northeast | 1.11% | 98.89% |
| The Midwest | 1.51% | 98.49% |
| The West | 1.69% | 98.31% |
| Abroad | 4.27% | 95.73% |
| Unknown | 0.00% | 100.00% |

**Table 1.5.8 Which of the following have you used in the past month? Midjourney. Broken out by year of class standing**

| Year of class standing | Yes | No |
|---|---|---|
| First year student | 1.26% | 98.74% |
| Sophomore | 1.67% | 98.33% |
| Junior | 1.17% | 98.83% |
| Senior | 2.71% | 97.29% |
| Unknown | 0.00% | 100.00% |

**Table 1.5.9 Which of the following have you used in the past month? Midjourney. Broken out by annual family of origin income level**

| Annual family of origin income level | Yes | No |
|---|---|---|
| Less than $50,000 per year | 2.55% | 97.45% |
| $50,000 to $90,000 per year | 1.36% | 98.64% |
| $90,000+ to $150,000 per year | 0.00% | 100.00% |
| $150,000+ to $250,000 per year | 4.81% | 95.19% |
| More than $250,000 per year | 0.00% | 100.00% |
| Unknown | 0.00% | 100.00% |

**Table 1.5.10 Which of the following have you used in the past month? Midjourney. Broken out by relationship with organized religion**

| Relationship with organized religion | Yes | No |
|---|---|---|
| I practice a religion thoroughly and consider my religion to be a very important part of my life. | 2.04% | 97.96% |
| I practice a religion and try to attend regular services and to participate as much as I can. | 2.55% | 97.45% |
| I identify with a religion but can't say I put a lot of effort into practicing it. | 1.09% | 98.91% |
| I don't really believe in or practice an organized religion. | 1.55% | 98.45% |
| Unknown | 0.00% | 100.00% |

**Table 1.5.11 Which of the following have you used in the past month? Midjourney. Broken out by political views**

| Political views | Yes | No |
|---|---|---|
| Very left wing | 1.99% | 98.01% |
| Liberal | 1.63% | 98.37% |
| Middle of the road | 1.79% | 98.21% |
| Conservative | 1.45% | 98.55% |
| Very right wing | 0.00% | 100.00% |
| Unknown | 0.00% | 100.00% |

**Table 1.5.12 Which of the following have you used in the past month? Midjourney. Broken out by college grades**

| College grades | Yes | No |
|---|---|---|
| A or A- average or more | 1.83% | 98.17% |
| B or B+ average | 1.66% | 98.34% |
| C or C+ or lower | 0.00% | 100.00% |
| Unknown | 0.00% | 100.00% |

### Table 1.5.13 Which of the following have you used in the past month? Midjourney. Broken out by academic major

| Academic major | Yes | No |
|---|---|---|
| Business, Economics or Finance | 0.00% | 100.00% |
| Psychology | 2.13% | 97.87% |
| Education or Library Science | 2.70% | 97.30% |
| Criminology/Law Enforcement | 0.00% | 100.00% |
| Occupational or Physical Therapy, Nursing, Public Health, Nutrition. other Health-Related | 0.93% | 99.07% |
| Communications, Media, Journalism | 0.00% | 100.00% |
| Fine Arts and Architecture | 4.76% | 95.24% |
| Music, Dance, Theater, other Performing Arts | 0.00% | 100.00% |
| English, Foreign Languages, Comp Literature, Creative Writing | 0.00% | 100.00% |
| Biology, Physics, Chemistry, Pre-Med | 1.50% | 98.50% |
| Geology, Oceanography, Environmental Sciences | 0.00% | 100.00% |
| Engineering, Mathematics, Computer Science | 3.47% | 96.53% |
| History, Classics | 0.00% | 100.00% |
| Sociology, Political Science, Anthropology or other Social Science, except Economics and Psychology | 0.00% | 100.00% |
| Other | 0.00% | 100.00% |

### Table 1.5.14 Which of the following have you used in the past month? Midjourney. Broken out by gender of respondent

| Gender of respondent | Yes | No |
|---|---|---|
| Male | 2.92% | 97.08% |
| Female | 0.97% | 99.03% |
| Transgender | 1.75% | 98.25% |
| Unknown | 0.00% | 100.00% |

### Table 1.5.15 Which of the following have you used in the past month? Midjourney. Broken out by status of current residency

| Status of current residency | Yes | No |
|---|---|---|
| At home with my parents or guardian | 2.26% | 97.74% |
| Off campus with others who are not my parents or guardian | 1.59% | 98.41% |
| Off campus alone | 0.87% | 99.13% |
| On campus in the dorms or college-provided suites | 1.62% | 98.38% |
| Unknown | 0.00% | 100.00% |

### Table 1.5.16 Which of the following have you used in the past month? Midjourney. Broken out by current employment situation

| Current employment situation | Yes | No |
|---|---|---|
| I don't have a full or part time job. | 1.93% | 98.07% |
| I have a part time job. | 1.56% | 98.44% |
| I have a full time job. | 1.32% | 98.68% |
| Unknown | 0.00% | 100.00% |

### Table 1.5.17 Which of the following have you used in the past month? Midjourney. Broken out by sexual orientation

| Sexual orientation | Yes | No |
|---|---|---|
| Heterosexual or "straight" | 1.53% | 98.47% |
| Homosexual or "gay" | 1.35% | 98.65% |
| Bi-sexual | 2.34% | 97.66% |
| Unknown | 0.00% | 100.00% |

Table 1.5.18 Which of the following have you used in the past month? Midjourney. Broken out by SAT or ACT score

| SAT or ACT score | Yes | No |
|---|---|---|
| 30 or over ACT or 1350 or over SAT | 0.80% | 99.20% |
| 24-29 ACT or 1170 to 1349 SAT | 1.56% | 98.44% |
| 20-23 ACT or 1050 to 1169 SAT | 1.11% | 98.89% |
| 17-19 ACT or 900 to 1050 SAT | 2.27% | 97.73% |
| 16 or Under ACT or Under 900 SAT | 3.70% | 96.30% |
| Never took either test | 2.88% | 97.12% |
| Unknown | 0.00% | 100.00% |

Table 1.5.19 Which of the following have you used in the past month? Midjourney. Broken out by race or ethnicity

| Race or ethnicity | Yes | No |
|---|---|---|
| White or Caucasian | 1.16% | 98.84% |
| Black or African American | 0.75% | 99.25% |
| Latino or Hispanic | 1.92% | 98.08% |
| Asian or Asian American | 2.25% | 97.75% |
| American Indigenous, Eskimo, Pacific Islander, Hawaiian Native | 0.00% | 100.00% |
| Mixed race | 5.63% | 94.37% |
| Unknown | 0.00% | 100.00% |

### Table 1.5.20 Which of the following have you used in the past month? Midjourney. Broken out by religion

| Religion | Yes | No |
|---|---|---|
| I do not practice or identify with an organized religion | 1.84% | 98.16% |
| Hinduism | 2.00% | 98.00% |
| Islam | 0.00% | 100.00% |
| Judaism | 0.00% | 100.00% |
| Mormon | 0.00% | 100.00% |
| Catholic | 1.48% | 98.52% |
| Lutheran | 6.25% | 93.75% |
| Baptist | 0.00% | 100.00% |
| Evangelical Protestant Christianity | 0.00% | 100.00% |
| Protestant Christianity | 2.00% | 98.00% |
| Orthodox Christianity | 0.00% | 100.00% |
| Buddhism | 0.00% | 100.00% |
| Non-Denominational Christianity | 2.70% | 97.30% |
| Other | 1.72% | 98.28% |

### Table 1.6.1 Which of the following have you used in the past month? Grok.

| | No Answer | Yes | No |
|---|---|---|---|
| Entire sample | 0.00% | 0.98% | 99.02% |

### Table 1.6.2 Which of the following have you used in the past month? Grok. Broken out by tuition of college attended

| Tuition of college attended | Yes | No |
|---|---|---|
| Less than $6,000 | 1.12% | 98.88% |
| $6,000+ - $12,000 | 1.22% | 98.78% |
| $12,000+ - $20,000 | 0.76% | 99.24% |
| More than $20,000 | 0.81% | 99.19% |

**Table 1.6.3 Which of the following have you used in the past month? Grok. Broken out by enrollment of college attended**

| Enrollment of college attended | Yes | No |
|---|---|---|
| Less than 5,000 | 0.79% | 99.21% |
| 5,000+ - 12,000 | 1.15% | 98.85% |
| 12,000+ - 22,900 | 0.85% | 99.15% |
| More than 22,900 | 1.09% | 98.91% |

**Table 1.6.4 Which of the following have you used in the past month? Grok. Broken out by public or private college**

| Public or private college | Yes | No |
|---|---|---|
| Public | 1.02% | 98.98% |
| Private | 0.85% | 99.15% |

**Table 1.6.5 Which of the following have you used in the past month? Grok. Broken out by age of respondent**

| Age of respondent | Yes | No |
|---|---|---|
| Under 19 | 0.26% | 99.74% |
| 19-21 | 0.42% | 99.58% |
| 22-27 | 1.42% | 98.58% |
| Over 28 | 2.58% | 97.42% |

**Table 1.6.6 Which of the following have you used in the past month? Grok. Broken out by urban, suburban or rural upbringing**

| Urban, suburban or rural upbringing | Yes | No |
|---|---|---|
| I grew up in a major city with more than 350,000 people | 1.52% | 98.48% |
| I grew up in a small or medium sized city with less than 350,000 people. | 1.18% | 98.82% |
| I grew up in a suburban area | 0.31% | 99.69% |
| I grew up in a rural area. | 1.11% | 98.89% |
| Unknown | 0.00% | 100.00% |

**Table 1.6.7 Which of the following have you used in the past month? Grok. Broken out by region of upbringing**

| Region of upbringing | Yes | No |
|---|---|---|
| The South | 0.00% | 100.00% |
| The Northeast | 1.11% | 98.89% |
| The Midwest | 0.75% | 99.25% |
| The West | 0.85% | 99.15% |
| Abroad | 3.05% | 96.95% |
| Unknown | 0.00% | 100.00% |

**Table 1.6.8 Which of the following have you used in the past month? Grok. Broken out by year of class standing**

| Year of class standing | Yes | No |
|---|---|---|
| First year student | 0.50% | 99.50% |
| Sophomore | 1.11% | 98.89% |
| Junior | 1.75% | 98.25% |
| Senior | 1.16% | 98.84% |
| Unknown | 0.00% | 100.00% |

**Table 1.6.9 Which of the following have you used in the past month? Grok. Broken out by annual family of origin income level**

| Annual family of origin income level | Yes | No |
|---|---|---|
| Less than $50,000 per year | 2.23% | 97.77% |
| $50,000 to $90,000 per year | 0.34% | 99.66% |
| $90,000+ to $150,000 per year | 0.00% | 100.00% |
| $150,000+ to $250,000 per year | 0.96% | 99.04% |
| More than $250,000 per year | 0.00% | 100.00% |
| Unknown | 4.55% | 95.45% |

**Table 1.6.10 Which of the following have you used in the past month? Grok. Broken out by relationship with organized religion**

| Relationship with organized religion | Yes | No |
|---|---|---|
| I practice a religion thoroughly and consider my religion to be a very important part of my life. | 2.04% | 97.96% |
| I practice a religion and try to attend regular services and to participate as much as I can. | 0.64% | 99.36% |
| I identify with a religion but can't say I put a lot of effort into practicing it. | 1.09% | 98.91% |
| I don't really believe in or practice an organized religion. | 0.26% | 99.74% |
| Unknown | 12.50% | 87.50% |

**Table 1.6.11 Which of the following have you used in the past month? Grok. Broken out by political views**

| Political views | Yes | No |
|---|---|---|
| Very left wing | 0.00% | 100.00% |
| Liberal | 1.08% | 98.92% |
| Middle of the road | 0.90% | 99.10% |
| Conservative | 2.17% | 97.83% |
| Very right wing | 0.00% | 100.00% |
| Unknown | 0.00% | 100.00% |

**Table 1.6.12 Which of the following have you used in the past month? Grok. Broken out by college grades**

| College grades | Yes | No |
|---|---|---|
| A or A- average or more | 1.07% | 98.93% |
| B or B+ average | 0.66% | 99.34% |
| C or C+ or lower | 1.61% | 98.39% |
| Unknown | 0.00% | 100.00% |

**Table 1.6.13 Which of the following have you used in the past month? Grok. Broken out by academic major**

| Academic major | Yes | No |
|---|---|---|
| Business, Economics or Finance | 0.79% | 99.21% |
| Psychology | 0.00% | 100.00% |
| Education or Library Science | 0.00% | 100.00% |
| Criminology/Law Enforcement | 0.00% | 100.00% |
| Occupational or Physical Therapy, Nursing, Public Health, Nutrition. other Health-Related | 0.93% | 99.07% |
| Communications, Media, Journalism | 0.00% | 100.00% |
| Fine Arts and Architecture | 0.00% | 100.00% |
| Music, Dance, Theater, other Performing Arts | 0.00% | 100.00% |
| English, Foreign Languages, Comp Literature, Creative Writing | 0.00% | 100.00% |
| Biology, Physics, Chemistry, Pre-Med | 0.75% | 99.25% |
| Geology, Oceanography, Environmental Sciences | 0.00% | 100.00% |
| Engineering, Mathematics, Computer Science | 2.97% | 97.03% |
| History, Classics | 7.69% | 92.31% |
| Sociology, Political Science, Anthropology or other Social Science, except Economics and Psychology | 0.00% | 100.00% |
| Other | 0.00% | 100.00% |

**Table 1.6.14 Which of the following have you used in the past month? Grok. Broken out by gender of respondent**

| Gender of respondent | Yes | No |
|---|---|---|
| Male | 2.34% | 97.66% |
| Female | 0.32% | 99.68% |
| Transgender | 0.00% | 100.00% |
| Unknown | 0.00% | 100.00% |

**Table 1.6.15 Which of the following have you used in the past month? Grok. Broken out by status of current residency**

| Status of current residency | Yes | No |
|---|---|---|
| At home with my parents or guardian | 0.45% | 99.55% |
| Off campus with others who are not my parents or guardian | 1.19% | 98.81% |
| Off campus alone | 1.74% | 98.26% |
| On campus in the dorms or college-provided suites | 0.93% | 99.07% |
| Unknown | 0.00% | 100.00% |

**Table 1.6.16 Which of the following have you used in the past month? Grok. Broken out by current employment situation**

| Current employment situation | Yes | No |
|---|---|---|
| I don't have a full or part time job. | 1.21% | 98.79% |
| I have a part time job. | 0.89% | 99.11% |
| I have a full time job. | 0.66% | 99.34% |
| Unknown | 0.00% | 100.00% |

**Table 1.6.17 Which of the following have you used in the past month? Grok. Broken out by sexual orientation**

| Sexual orientation | Yes | No |
|---|---|---|
| Heterosexual or "straight" | 1.25% | 98.75% |
| Homosexual or "gay" | 1.35% | 98.65% |
| Bi-sexual | 0.00% | 100.00% |
| Unknown | 0.00% | 100.00% |

### Table 1.6.18 Which of the following have you used in the past month? Grok. Broken out by SAT or ACT score

| SAT or ACT score | Yes | No |
|---|---|---|
| 30 or over ACT or 1350 or over SAT | 1.20% | 98.80% |
| 24-29 ACT or 1170 to 1349 SAT | 0.39% | 99.61% |
| 20-23 ACT or 1050 to 1169 SAT | 0.56% | 99.44% |
| 17-19 ACT or 900 to 1050 SAT | 0.00% | 100.00% |
| 16 or Under ACT or Under 900 SAT | 0.00% | 100.00% |
| Never took either test | 2.40% | 97.60% |
| Unknown | 0.00% | 100.00% |

### Table 1.6.19 Which of the following have you used in the past month? Grok. Broken out by race or ethnicity

| Race or ethnicity | Yes | No |
|---|---|---|
| White or Caucasian | 0.77% | 99.23% |
| Black or African American | 1.50% | 98.50% |
| Latino or Hispanic | 0.00% | 100.00% |
| Asian or Asian American | 1.69% | 98.31% |
| American Indigenous, Eskimo, Pacific Islander, Hawaiian Native | 0.00% | 100.00% |
| Mixed race | 0.00% | 100.00% |
| Unknown | 8.33% | 91.67% |

Table 1.6.20 Which of the following have you used in the past month? Grok. Broken out by religion

| Religion | Yes | No |
|---|---|---|
| I do not practice or identify with an organized religion | 0.79% | 99.21% |
| Hinduism | 2.00% | 98.00% |
| Islam | 4.17% | 95.83% |
| Judaism | 3.70% | 96.30% |
| Mormon | 0.00% | 100.00% |
| Catholic | 0.74% | 99.26% |
| Lutheran | 0.00% | 100.00% |
| Baptist | 0.00% | 100.00% |
| Evangelical Protestant Christianity | 0.00% | 100.00% |
| Protestant Christianity | 4.00% | 96.00% |
| Orthodox Christianity | 0.00% | 100.00% |
| Buddhism | 0.00% | 100.00% |
| Non-Denominational Christianity | 0.00% | 100.00% |
| Other | 0.00% | 100.00% |

Other AI Applications Mentioned by Survey Participants:

1) None
2) None
3) None of the above
4) None
5) None
6) None
7) None
8) None
9) Photoshop generative AI
10) Snapchat
11) None
12) None
13) None
14) I haven't used AI
15) Einstein AI
16) Adobe Firefly
17) None
18) Galaxy AI
19) Suno, Luma Dream Machine
20) NotebookLM
21) LMNotebook
22) Google

23) None
24) None
25) None
26) None
27) Google
28) Google
29) iAsk.ai
30) None
31) None
32) None
33) Google thesaurus
34) None
35) Perplexity
36) None of these.
37) None
38) Snapchats ai and Facebook too
39) None
40) Liner
41) None
42) None
43) None
44) None
45) None
46) Duck Duck Go, Safari, ChatOn
47) Adobe Photoshop
48) Magic school ai
49) I do not use AI. The only time is when I google personal life situations, I have that I may need an answer to.
50) None
51) None
52) Aria (Opera GX)
53) NotebookLM
54) None
55) None
56) Aria AI
57) MagicSchool
58) Microsoft teams and colleague portal
59) Perplexity AI
60) Perplexity
61) None, and I've also been asked to disable Copilot by CMMC clients.
62) None
63) I haven't used ai
64) None
65) Character AI
66) Google AI
67) Snapchat ai
68) Character.AI
69) None
70) EggnogAI

71) School ai
72) Grammarly
73) None
74) Neither
75) None
76) None
77) MagicSchool AI
78) I do not use generative AI.
79) Whoop AI
80) None
81) None
82) None
83) Grammarly
84) Snapchat ai
85) Google
86) None.
87) None
88) None
89) Snapchat AI
90) None
91) Black box ai ,you ai
92) AI Grammarly
93) Feynman
94) None
95) None
96) Aria
97) None
98) None
99) None
100) Quillbot
101) Just done
102) None
103) Adobe Firefly
104) None
105) Perplexity
106) Perplexity (AI search engine)
107) Perplexity
108) None
109) GitHub Copilot
110) Snapchat AI
111) Perplexity
112) None
113) Perplexity
114) Perplexity
115) None
116) None
117) None
118) None
119) Perplexity

120) Elicit
121) Perplexity
122) GitHub copilot

# Table 2 In the past week about how much time, in minutes, have you spent using the artificial intelligence applications listed below, or similar such applications?

### Table 2.1.1 In the past week about how much time, in minutes, have you spent using the artificial intelligence applications listed below, or similar such applications? ChatGPT

| | Mean | Median | Minimum | Maximum |
|---|---|---|---|---|
| Entire sample | 34.99 | 0.00 | 0.00 | 3800.00 |

### Table 2.1.2 In the past week about how much time, in minutes, have you spent using the artificial intelligence applications listed below, or similar such applications? ChatGPT Broken out by tuition of college attended

| Tuition of college attended | Mean | Median | Minimum | Maximum |
|---|---|---|---|---|
| Less than $6,000 | 17.81 | 0.00 | 0.00 | 600.00 |
| $6,000+ - $12,000 | 46.44 | 0.00 | 0.00 | 3800.00 |
| $12,000+ - $20,000 | 31.04 | 0.00 | 0.00 | 960.00 |
| More than $20,000 | 46.33 | 5.00 | 0.00 | 3360.00 |

### Table 2.1.3 In the past week about how much time, in minutes, have you spent using the artificial intelligence applications listed below, or similar such applications? ChatGPT Broken out by enrollment of college attended

| Enrollment of college attended | Mean | Median | Minimum | Maximum |
|---|---|---|---|---|
| Less than 5,000 | 43.67 | 5.00 | 0.00 | 3360.00 |
| 5,000+ - 12,000 | 50.03 | 0.00 | 0.00 | 3800.00 |
| 12,000+ - 22,900 | 27.99 | 0.00 | 0.00 | 600.00 |
| More than 22,900 | 18.82 | 0.00 | 0.00 | 600.00 |

**Table 2.1.4 In the past week about how much time, in minutes, have you spent using the artificial intelligence applications listed below, or similar such applications? ChatGPT Broken out by public or private college**

| Public or private college | Mean | Median | Minimum | Maximum |
|---|---|---|---|---|
| Public | 31.58 | 0.00 | 0.00 | 3800.00 |
| Private | 46.47 | 5.00 | 0.00 | 3360.00 |

**Table 2.1.5 In the past week about how much time, in minutes, have you spent using the artificial intelligence applications listed below, or similar such applications? ChatGPT Broken out by age of respondent**

| Age of respondent | Mean | Median | Minimum | Maximum |
|---|---|---|---|---|
| Under 19 | 29.05 | 0.00 | 0.00 | 3360.00 |
| 19-21 | 47.66 | 0.00 | 0.00 | 3800.00 |
| 22-27 | 35.24 | 0.00 | 0.00 | 600.00 |
| Over 28 | 30.77 | 0.00 | 0.00 | 960.00 |

**Table 2.1.6 In the past week about how much time, in minutes, have you spent using the artificial intelligence applications listed below, or similar such applications? ChatGPT Broken out by urban. suburban or rural upbringing**

| Urban, suburban or rural upbringing | Mean | Median | Minimum | Maximum |
|---|---|---|---|---|
| I grew up in a major city with more than 350,000 people | 55.81 | 5.00 | 0.00 | 3360.00 |
| I grew up in a small or medium sized city with less than 350,000 people. | 43.97 | 0.00 | 0.00 | 3800.00 |
| I grew up in a suburban area | 21.75 | 0.00 | 0.00 | 600.00 |
| I grew up in a rural area. | 16.26 | 0.00 | 0.00 | 300.00 |
| Unknown | 1.67 | 0.00 | 0.00 | 10.00 |

**Table 2.1.7 In the past week about how much time, in minutes, have you spent using the artificial intelligence applications listed below, or similar such applications? ChatGPT Broken out by region of upbringing**

| Region of upbringing | Mean | Median | Minimum | Maximum |
|---|---|---|---|---|
| The South | 23.29 | 0.00 | 0.00 | 960.00 |
| The Northeast | 21.99 | 0.00 | 0.00 | 300.00 |
| The Midwest | 28.79 | 0.00 | 0.00 | 3800.00 |
| The West | 23.90 | 4.00 | 0.00 | 400.00 |
| Abroad | 84.12 | 10.00 | 0.00 | 3360.00 |
| Unknown | 0.00 | 0.00 | 0.00 | 0.00 |

**Table 2.1.8 In the past week about how much time, in minutes, have you spent using the artificial intelligence applications listed below, or similar such applications? ChatGPT Broken out by year of class standing**

| Year of class standing | Mean | Median | Minimum | Maximum |
|---|---|---|---|---|
| First year student | 27.19 | 0.00 | 0.00 | 960.00 |
| Sophomore | 40.32 | 0.00 | 0.00 | 3360.00 |
| Junior | 46.75 | 0.00 | 0.00 | 3800.00 |
| Senior | 36.55 | 0.00 | 0.00 | 600.00 |
| Unknown | 17.38 | 0.00 | 0.00 | 200.00 |

**Table 2.1.9 In the past week about how much time, in minutes, have you spent using the artificial intelligence applications listed below, or similar such applications? ChatGPT Broken out by annual family of origin income level**

| Annual family of origin income level | Mean | Median | Minimum | Maximum |
|---|---|---|---|---|
| Less than $50,000 per year | 47.15 | 0.00 | 0.00 | 3800.00 |
| $50,000 to $90,000 per year | 23.54 | 0.00 | 0.00 | 600.00 |
| $90,000+ to $150,000 per year | 25.66 | 0.00 | 0.00 | 960.00 |
| $150,000+ to $250,000 per year | 32.56 | 0.50 | 0.00 | 300.00 |
| More than $250,000 per year | 58.62 | 2.50 | 0.00 | 3360.00 |
| Unknown | 12.95 | 0.00 | 0.00 | 180.00 |

**Table 2.1.10 In the past week about how much time, in minutes, have you spent using the artificial intelligence applications listed below, or similar such applications? ChatGPT Broken out by relationship with organized religion**

| Relationship with organized religion | Mean | Median | Minimum | Maximum |
|---|---|---|---|---|
| I practice a religion thoroughly and consider my religion to be a very important part of my life. | 33.16 | 0.00 | 0.00 | 600.00 |
| I practice a religion and try to attend regular services and to participate as much as I can. | 47.37 | 0.00 | 0.00 | 3800.00 |
| I identify with a religion but can't say I put a lot of effort into practicing it. | 42.91 | 0.00 | 0.00 | 3360.00 |
| I don't really believe in or practice an organized religion. | 25.61 | 0.00 | 0.00 | 800.00 |
| Unknown | 18.75 | 0.00 | 0.00 | 150.00 |

**Table 2.1.11 In the past week about how much time, in minutes, have you spent using the artificial intelligence applications listed below, or similar such applications? ChatGPT Broken out by political views**

| Political views | Mean | Median | Minimum | Maximum |
|---|---|---|---|---|
| Very left wing | 10.68 | 0.00 | 0.00 | 180.00 |
| Liberal | 47.08 | 0.00 | 0.00 | 3800.00 |
| Middle of the road | 28.63 | 0.00 | 0.00 | 600.00 |
| Conservative | 48.36 | 0.00 | 0.00 | 3360.00 |
| Very right wing | 24.20 | 0.00 | 0.00 | 180.00 |
| Unknown | 2.22 | 0.00 | 0.00 | 20.00 |

**Table 2.1.12 In the past week about how much time, in minutes, have you spent using the artificial intelligence applications listed below, or similar such applications? ChatGPT Broken out by college grades**

| College grades | Mean | Median | Minimum | Maximum |
|---|---|---|---|---|
| A or A- average or more | 36.40 | 0.00 | 0.00 | 3360.00 |
| B or B+ average | 35.00 | 0.00 | 0.00 | 3800.00 |
| C or C+ or lower | 22.27 | 0.00 | 0.00 | 600.00 |
| Unknown | 0.00 | 0.00 | 0.00 | 0.00 |

**Table 2.1.13 In the past week about how much time, in minutes, have you spent using the artificial intelligence applications listed below, or similar such applications? ChatGPT Broken out by academic major**

| Academic major | Mean | Median | Minimum | Maximum |
|---|---|---|---|---|
| Business, Economics or Finance | 28.25 | 2.50 | 0.00 | 400.00 |
| Psychology | 62.60 | 0.00 | 0.00 | 3800.00 |
| Education or Library Science | 12.82 | 0.00 | 0.00 | 120.00 |
| Criminology/Law Enforcement | 5.80 | 0.00 | 0.00 | 60.00 |
| Occupational or Physical Therapy, Nursing, Public Health, Nutrition. other Health-Related | 23.36 | 0.00 | 0.00 | 600.00 |
| Communications, Media, Journalism | 46.33 | 3.00 | 0.00 | 600.00 |
| Fine Arts and Architecture | 14.33 | 0.00 | 0.00 | 180.00 |
| Music, Dance, Theater, other Performing Arts | 8.46 | 0.00 | 0.00 | 120.00 |
| English,Foreign Languages, Comp Literature, Creative Writing | 6.97 | 0.00 | 0.00 | 40.00 |
| Biology, Physics, Chemistry, Pre-Med | 34.29 | 0.00 | 0.00 | 500.00 |
| Geology, Oceanography, Environmental Sciences | 19.42 | 0.00 | 0.00 | 420.00 |
| Engineering, Mathematics, Computer Science | 51.34 | 10.00 | 0.00 | 800.00 |
| History, Classics | 6.54 | 0.00 | 0.00 | 60.00 |
| Sociology, Political Science, Anthropology or other Social Science, except Economics and Psychology | 62.56 | 0.00 | 0.00 | 3360.00 |
| Other | 3.15 | 0.00 | 0.00 | 30.00 |

**Table 2.1.14 In the past week about how much time, in minutes, have you spent using the artificial intelligence applications listed below, or similar such applications? ChatGPT Broken out by gender of respondent**

| Gender of respondent | Mean | Median | Minimum | Maximum |
|---|---|---|---|---|
| Male | 33.42 | 5.00 | 0.00 | 500.00 |
| Female | 38.19 | 0.00 | 0.00 | 3800.00 |
| Transgender | 11.32 | 0.00 | 0.00 | 150.00 |
| Unknown | 0.67 | 0.00 | 0.00 | 2.00 |

**Table 2.1.15 In the past week about how much time, in minutes, have you spent using the artificial intelligence applications listed below, or similar such applications? ChatGPT Broken out by status of current residency**

| Status of current residency | Mean | Median | Minimum | Maximum |
|---|---|---|---|---|
| At home with my parents or guardian | 20.34 | 0.00 | 0.00 | 360.00 |
| Off campus with others who are not my parents or guardian | 26.82 | 0.00 | 0.00 | 600.00 |
| Off campus alone | 47.97 | 0.00 | 0.00 | 960.00 |
| On campus in the dorms or college-provided suites | 44.05 | 0.00 | 0.00 | 3800.00 |
| Unknown | 0.00 | 0.00 | 0.00 | 0.00 |

**Table 2.1.16 In the past week about how much time, in minutes, have you spent using the artificial intelligence applications listed below, or similar such applications? ChatGPT Broken out by current employment situation**

| Current employment situation | Mean | Median | Minimum | Maximum |
|---|---|---|---|---|
| I don't have a full or part time job. | 44.73 | 0.00 | 0.00 | 3800.00 |
| I have a part time job. | 32.65 | 0.00 | 0.00 | 960.00 |
| I have a full time job. | 16.71 | 0.00 | 0.00 | 360.00 |
| Unknown | 0.83 | 0.00 | 0.00 | 5.00 |

**Table 2.1.17 In the past week about how much time, in minutes, have you spent using the artificial intelligence applications listed below, or similar such applications? ChatGPT Broken out by sexual orientation**

| Sexual orientation | Mean | Median | Minimum | Maximum |
|---|---|---|---|---|
| Heterosexual or "straight" | 41.25 | 0.00 | 0.00 | 3800.00 |
| Homosexual or "gay" | 29.35 | 0.00 | 0.00 | 960.00 |
| Bi-sexual | 16.69 | 0.00 | 0.00 | 300.00 |
| Unknown | 23.67 | 0.00 | 0.00 | 240.00 |

**Table 2.1.18 In the past week about how much time, in minutes, have you spent using the artificial intelligence applications listed below, or similar such applications? ChatGPT Broken out by SAT or ACT score**

| SAT or ACT score | Mean | Median | Minimum | Maximum |
|---|---|---|---|---|
| 30 or over ACT or 1350 or over SAT | 44.58 | 2.00 | 0.00 | 3360.00 |
| 24-29 ACT or 1170 to 1349 SAT | 35.42 | 0.00 | 0.00 | 3800.00 |
| 20-23 ACT or 1050 to 1169 SAT | 25.11 | 0.00 | 0.00 | 600.00 |
| 17-19 ACT or 900 to 1050 SAT | 11.74 | 0.00 | 0.00 | 180.00 |
| 16 or Under ACT or Under 900 SAT | 18.85 | 0.00 | 0.00 | 180.00 |
| Never took either test | 45.14 | 0.00 | 0.00 | 960.00 |
| Unknown | 0.91 | 0.00 | 0.00 | 5.00 |

**Table 2.1.19 In the past week about how much time, in minutes, have you spent using the artificial intelligence applications listed below, or similar such applications? ChatGPT Broken out by race or ethnicity**

| Race or ethnicity | Mean | Median | Minimum | Maximum |
|---|---|---|---|---|
| White or Caucasian | 19.74 | 0.00 | 0.00 | 960.00 |
| Black or African American | 60.39 | 0.00 | 0.00 | 3800.00 |
| Latino or Hispanic | 27.56 | 2.00 | 0.00 | 200.00 |
| Asian or Asian American | 73.26 | 10.00 | 0.00 | 3360.00 |
| American indigenous, eskimo, pacific islander, Hawaiian native | 12.00 | 0.00 | 0.00 | 60.00 |
| Mixed race | 21.34 | 0.00 | 0.00 | 500.00 |
| Unknown | 0.00 | 0.00 | 0.00 | 0.00 |

**Table 2.1.20 In the past week about how much time, in minutes, have you spent using the artificial intelligence applications listed below, or similar such applications? ChatGPT Broken out by religion**

| Religion | Mean | Median | Minimum | Maximum |
|---|---|---|---|---|
| I do not practice or identify with an organized religion | 25.67 | 0.00 | 0.00 | 500.00 |
| Hinduism | 51.37 | 0.00 | 0.00 | 600.00 |
| Islam | 52.42 | 0.00 | 0.00 | 400.00 |
| Judaism | 49.41 | 4.00 | 0.00 | 800.00 |
| Mormon | 7.83 | 0.00 | 0.00 | 45.00 |
| Catholic | 59.53 | 5.00 | 0.00 | 3800.00 |
| Lutheran | 22.09 | 0.00 | 0.00 | 210.00 |
| Baptist | 11.65 | 0.00 | 0.00 | 180.00 |
| Evangelical Protestant Christianity | 53.70 | 10.00 | 0.00 | 600.00 |
| Protestant Christianity | 18.64 | 0.00 | 0.00 | 180.00 |
| Orthodox Christianity | 26.11 | 5.00 | 0.00 | 180.00 |
| Buddhism | 195.50 | 30.00 | 0.00 | 3360.00 |
| Non-Denominational Christianity | 16.22 | 0.00 | 0.00 | 300.00 |
| Other | 29.05 | 0.00 | 0.00 | 600.00 |

**Table 2.2.1 In the past week about how much time, in minutes, have you spent using the artificial intelligence applications listed below, or similar such applications? Gemini.**

| | Mean | Median | Minimum | Maximum |
|---|---|---|---|---|
| Entire sample | 4.84 | 0.00 | 0.00 | 670.00 |

**Table 2.2.2 In the past week about how much time, in minutes, have you spent using the artificial intelligence applications listed below, or similar such applications? Gemini. Broken out by tuition of college attended**

| Tuition of college attended | Mean | Median | Minimum | Maximum |
|---|---|---|---|---|
| Less than $6,000 | 2.18 | 0.00 | 0.00 | 150.00 |
| $6,000+ - $12,000 | 9.98 | 0.00 | 0.00 | 600.00 |
| $12,000+ - $20,000 | 5.05 | 0.00 | 0.00 | 670.00 |
| More than $20,000 | 2.38 | 0.00 | 0.00 | 200.00 |

**Table 2.2.3 In the past week about how much time, in minutes, have you spent using the artificial intelligence applications listed below, or similar such applications? Gemini. Broken out by enrollment of college attended**

| Enrollment of college attended | Mean | Median | Minimum | Maximum |
|---|---|---|---|---|
| Less than 5,000 | 2.62 | 0.00 | 0.00 | 200.00 |
| 5,000+ - 12,000 | 9.49 | 0.00 | 0.00 | 670.00 |
| 12,000+ - 22,900 | 5.18 | 0.00 | 0.00 | 600.00 |
| More than 22,900 | 2.21 | 0.00 | 0.00 | 150.00 |

**Table 2.2.4 In the past week about how much time, in minutes, have you spent using the artificial intelligence applications listed below, or similar such applications? Gemini. Broken out by public or private college**

| Public or private college | Mean | Median | Minimum | Maximum |
|---|---|---|---|---|
| Public | 5.53 | 0.00 | 0.00 | 670.00 |
| Private | 2.52 | 0.00 | 0.00 | 200.00 |

**Table 2.2.5 In the past week about how much time, in minutes, have you spent using the artificial intelligence applications listed below, or similar such applications? Gemini. Broken out by age of respondent**

| Age of respondent | Mean | Median | Minimum | Maximum |
|---|---|---|---|---|
| Under 19 | 5.61 | 0.00 | 0.00 | 670.00 |
| 19-21 | 2.53 | 0.00 | 0.00 | 200.00 |
| 22-27 | 5.08 | 0.00 | 0.00 | 500.00 |
| Over 28 | 5.93 | 0.00 | 0.00 | 600.00 |

**Table 2.2.6 In the past week about how much time, in minutes, have you spent using the artificial intelligence applications listed below, or similar such applications? Gemini. Broken out by urban, suburban or rural upbringing**

| Urban, suburban or rural upbringing | Mean | Median | Minimum | Maximum |
|---|---|---|---|---|
| I grew up in a major city with more than 350,000 people | 8.54 | 0.00 | 0.00 | 600.00 |
| I grew up in a small or medium sized city with less than 350,000 people. | 2.76 | 0.00 | 0.00 | 300.00 |
| I grew up in a suburban area | 3.18 | 0.00 | 0.00 | 480.00 |
| I grew up in a rural area. | 5.47 | 0.00 | 0.00 | 670.00 |
| Unknown | 0.00 | 0.00 | 0.00 | 0.00 |

**Table 2.2.7 In the past week about how much time, in minutes, have you spent using the artificial intelligence applications listed below, or similar such applications? Gemini. Broken out by region of upbringing**

| Region of upbringing | Mean | Median | Minimum | Maximum |
|---|---|---|---|---|
| The South | 2.26 | 0.00 | 0.00 | 180.00 |
| The Northeast | 6.11 | 0.00 | 0.00 | 300.00 |
| The Midwest | 2.54 | 0.00 | 0.00 | 480.00 |
| The West | 1.53 | 0.00 | 0.00 | 60.00 |
| Abroad | 16.19 | 0.00 | 0.00 | 670.00 |
| Unknown | 0.00 | 0.00 | 0.00 | 0.00 |

**Table 2.2.8 In the past week about how much time, in minutes, have you spent using the artificial intelligence applications listed below, or similar such applications? Gemini. Broken out by year of class standing**

| Year of class standing | Mean | Median | Minimum | Maximum |
|---|---|---|---|---|
| First year student | 5.44 | 0.00 | 0.00 | 670.00 |
| Sophomore | 1.35 | 0.00 | 0.00 | 60.00 |
| Junior | 2.79 | 0.00 | 0.00 | 200.00 |
| Senior | 7.84 | 0.00 | 0.00 | 600.00 |
| Unknown | 3.13 | 0.00 | 0.00 | 50.00 |

**Table 2.2.9 In the past week about how much time, in minutes, have you spent using the artificial intelligence applications listed below, or similar such applications? Gemini. Broken out by annual family of origin income level**

| Annual family of origin income level | Mean | Median | Minimum | Maximum |
|---|---|---|---|---|
| Less than $50,000 per year | 9.65 | 0.00 | 0.00 | 670.00 |
| $50,000 to $90,000 per year | 3.56 | 0.00 | 0.00 | 480.00 |
| $90,000+ to $150,000 per year | 2.19 | 0.00 | 0.00 | 120.00 |
| $150,000+ to $250,000 per year | 3.69 | 0.00 | 0.00 | 180.00 |
| More than $250,000 per year | 0.33 | 0.00 | 0.00 | 15.00 |
| Unknown | 1.14 | 0.00 | 0.00 | 25.00 |

**Table 2.2.10 In the past week about how much time, in minutes, have you spent using the artificial intelligence applications listed below, or similar such applications? Gemini. Broken out by relationship with organized religion**

| Relationship with organized religion | Mean | Median | Minimum | Maximum |
|---|---|---|---|---|
| I practice a religion thoroughly and consider my religion to be a very important part of my life. | 5.00 | 0.00 | 0.00 | 600.00 |
| I practice a religion and try to attend regular services and to participate as much as I can. | 5.34 | 0.00 | 0.00 | 480.00 |
| I identify with a religion but can't say I put a lot of effort into practicing it. | 5.99 | 0.00 | 0.00 | 670.00 |
| I don't really believe in or practice an organized religion. | 3.84 | 0.00 | 0.00 | 300.00 |
| Unknown | 0.63 | 0.00 | 0.00 | 5.00 |

**Table 2.2.11 In the past week about how much time, in minutes, have you spent using the artificial intelligence applications listed below, or similar such applications? Gemini. Broken out by political views**

| Political views | Mean | Median | Minimum | Maximum |
|---|---|---|---|---|
| Very left wing | 1.42 | 0.00 | 0.00 | 90.00 |
| Liberal | 5.94 | 0.00 | 0.00 | 670.00 |
| Middle of the road | 5.54 | 0.00 | 0.00 | 480.00 |
| Conservative | 5.00 | 0.00 | 0.00 | 600.00 |
| Very right wing | 0.00 | 0.00 | 0.00 | 0.00 |
| Unknown | 0.00 | 0.00 | 0.00 | 0.00 |

**Table 2.2.12 In the past week about how much time, in minutes, have you spent using the artificial intelligence applications listed below, or similar such applications? Gemini. Broken out by college grades**

| College grades | Mean | Median | Minimum | Maximum |
|---|---|---|---|---|
| A or A- average or more | 4.34 | 0.00 | 0.00 | 600.00 |
| B or B+ average | 6.88 | 0.00 | 0.00 | 670.00 |
| C or C+ or lower | 0.56 | 0.00 | 0.00 | 15.00 |
| Unknown | 0.00 | 0.00 | 0.00 | 0.00 |

**Table 2.2.13 In the past week about how much time, in minutes, have you spent using the artificial intelligence applications listed below, or similar such applications? Gemini. Broken out by academic major**

| Academic major | Mean | Median | Minimum | Maximum |
|---|---|---|---|---|
| Business, Economics or Finance | 1.85 | 0.00 | 0.00 | 60.00 |
| Psychology | 1.32 | 0.00 | 0.00 | 64.00 |
| Education or Library Science | 1.50 | 0.00 | 0.00 | 30.00 |
| Criminology/Law Enforcement | 0.33 | 0.00 | 0.00 | 5.00 |
| Occupational or Physical Therapy, Nursing, Public Health, Nutrition. other Health-Related | 6.44 | 0.00 | 0.00 | 600.00 |
| Communications, Media, Journalism | 2.71 | 0.00 | 0.00 | 60.00 |
| Fine Arts and Architecture | 5.87 | 0.00 | 0.00 | 300.00 |
| Music, Dance, Theater, other Performing Arts | 0.00 | 0.00 | 0.00 | 0.00 |
| English, Foreign Languages, Comp Literature, Creative Writing | 18.62 | 0.00 | 0.00 | 480.00 |
| Biology, Physics, Chemistry, Pre-Med | 9.82 | 0.00 | 0.00 | 670.00 |
| Geology, Oceanography, Environmental Sciences | 2.31 | 0.00 | 0.00 | 60.00 |
| Engineering, Mathematics, Computer Science | 6.25 | 0.00 | 0.00 | 200.00 |
| History, Classics | 0.00 | 0.00 | 0.00 | 0.00 |
| Sociology, Political Science, Anthropology or other Social Science, except Economics and Psychology | 2.33 | 0.00 | 0.00 | 60.00 |
| Other | 0.00 | 0.00 | 0.00 | 0.00 |

**Table 2.2.14 In the past week about how much time, in minutes, have you spent using the artificial intelligence applications listed below, or similar such applications? Gemini. Broken out by gender of respondent**

| Gender of respondent | Mean | Median | Minimum | Maximum |
|---|---|---|---|---|
| Male | 9.65 | 0.00 | 0.00 | 670.00 |
| Female | 2.36 | 0.00 | 0.00 | 600.00 |
| Transgender | 3.23 | 0.00 | 0.00 | 64.00 |
| Unknown | 0.00 | 0.00 | 0.00 | 0.00 |

**Table 2.2.15 In the past week about how much time, in minutes, have you spent using the artificial intelligence applications listed below, or similar such applications? Gemini. Broken out by status of current residency**

| Status of current residency | Mean | Median | Minimum | Maximum |
|---|---|---|---|---|
| At home with my parents or guardian | 3.96 | 0.00 | 0.00 | 480.00 |
| Off campus with others who are not my parents or guardian | 2.30 | 0.00 | 0.00 | 150.00 |
| Off campus alone | 14.26 | 0.00 | 0.00 | 600.00 |
| On campus in the dorms or college-provided suites | 4.30 | 0.00 | 0.00 | 670.00 |
| Unknown | 0.00 | 0.00 | 0.00 | 0.00 |

**Table 2.2.16 In the past week about how much time, in minutes, have you spent using the artificial intelligence applications listed below, or similar such applications? Gemini. Broken out by current employment situation**

| Current employment situation | Mean | Median | Minimum | Maximum |
|---|---|---|---|---|
| I don't have a full or part time job. | 7.59 | 0.00 | 0.00 | 670.00 |
| I have a part time job. | 2.94 | 0.00 | 0.00 | 300.00 |
| I have a full time job. | 3.19 | 0.00 | 0.00 | 150.00 |
| Unknown | 0.00 | 0.00 | 0.00 | 0.00 |

**Table 2.2.17 In the past week about how much time, in minutes, have you spent using the artificial intelligence applications listed below, or similar such applications? Gemini. Broken out by sexual orientation**

| Sexual orientation | Mean | Median | Minimum | Maximum |
|---|---|---|---|---|
| Heterosexual or "straight" | 4.86 | 0.00 | 0.00 | 600.00 |
| Homosexual or "gay" | 1.03 | 0.00 | 0.00 | 45.00 |
| Bi-sexual | 6.41 | 0.00 | 0.00 | 670.00 |
| Unknown | 0.67 | 0.00 | 0.00 | 10.00 |

**Table 2.2.18 In the past week about how much time, in minutes, have you spent using the artificial intelligence applications listed below, or similar such applications? Gemini. Broken out by SAT or ACT score**

| SAT or ACT score | Mean | Median | Minimum | Maximum |
|---|---|---|---|---|
| 30 or over ACT or 1350 or over SAT | 2.66 | 0.00 | 0.00 | 200.00 |
| 24-29 ACT or 1170 to 1349 SAT | 1.10 | 0.00 | 0.00 | 60.00 |
| 20-23 ACT or 1050 to 1169 SAT | 6.68 | 0.00 | 0.00 | 670.00 |
| 17-19 ACT or 900 to 1050 SAT | 2.51 | 0.00 | 0.00 | 64.00 |
| 16 or Under ACT or Under 900 SAT | 30.37 | 0.00 | 0.00 | 480.00 |
| Never took either test | 8.44 | 0.00 | 0.00 | 600.00 |
| Unknown | 0.09 | 0.00 | 0.00 | 1.00 |

**Table 2.2.19 In the past week about how much time, in minutes, have you spent using the artificial intelligence applications listed below, or similar such applications? Gemini. Broken out by race or ethnicity**

| Race or ethnicity | Mean | Median | Minimum | Maximum |
|---|---|---|---|---|
| White or Caucasian | 3.68 | 0.00 | 0.00 | 480.00 |
| Black or African American | 7.90 | 0.00 | 0.00 | 600.00 |
| Latino or Hispanic | 7.80 | 0.00 | 0.00 | 670.00 |
| Asian or Asian American | 6.52 | 0.00 | 0.00 | 500.00 |
| American Indigenous, Eskimo, Pacific Islander, Hawaiian Native | 0.00 | 0.00 | 0.00 | 0.00 |
| Mixed race | 0.28 | 0.00 | 0.00 | 10.00 |
| Unknown | 0.00 | 0.00 | 0.00 | 0.00 |

**Table 2.2.20 In the past week about how much time, in minutes, have you spent using the artificial intelligence applications listed below, or similar such applications? Gemini. Broken out by religion**

| Religion | Mean | Median | Minimum | Maximum |
|---|---|---|---|---|
| I do not practice or identify with an organized religion | 2.80 | 0.00 | 0.00 | 300.00 |
| Hinduism | 12.94 | 0.00 | 0.00 | 500.00 |
| Islam | 5.73 | 0.00 | 0.00 | 60.00 |
| Judaism | 0.00 | 0.00 | 0.00 | 0.00 |
| Mormon | 0.00 | 0.00 | 0.00 | 0.00 |
| Catholic | 8.63 | 0.00 | 0.00 | 670.00 |
| Lutheran | 2.84 | 0.00 | 0.00 | 50.00 |
| Baptist | 0.06 | 0.00 | 0.00 | 2.00 |
| Evangelical Protestant Christianity | 27.61 | 0.00 | 0.00 | 600.00 |
| Protestant Christianity | 11.50 | 0.00 | 0.00 | 480.00 |
| Orthodox Christianity | 6.11 | 0.00 | 0.00 | 100.00 |
| Buddhism | 0.25 | 0.00 | 0.00 | 5.00 |
| Non-Denominational Christianity | 2.75 | 0.00 | 0.00 | 180.00 |
| Other | 1.21 | 0.00 | 0.00 | 25.00 |

**Table 2.3.1 In the past week about how much time, in minutes, have you spent using the artificial intelligence applications listed below, or similar such applications? CoPilot.**

| | Mean | Median | Minimum | Maximum |
|---|---|---|---|---|
| Entire sample | 4.02 | 0.00 | 0.00 | 1000.00 |

**Table 2.3.2 In the past week about how much time, in minutes, have you spent using the artificial intelligence applications listed below, or similar such applications? CoPilot. Broken out by tuition of college attended**

| Tuition of college attended | Mean | Median | Minimum | Maximum |
|---|---|---|---|---|
| Less than $6,000 | 4.16 | 0.00 | 0.00 | 300.00 |
| $6,000+ - $12,000 | 7.76 | 0.00 | 0.00 | 1000.00 |
| $12,000+ - $20,000 | 3.34 | 0.00 | 0.00 | 120.00 |
| More than $20,000 | 0.89 | 0.00 | 0.00 | 120.00 |

**Table 2.3.3 In the past week about how much time, in minutes, have you spent using the artificial intelligence applications listed below, or similar such applications? CoPilot. Broken out by enrollment of college attended**

| Enrollment of college attended | Mean | Median | Minimum | Maximum |
|---|---|---|---|---|
| Less than 5,000 | 1.01 | 0.00 | 0.00 | 120.00 |
| 5,000+ - 12,000 | 7.96 | 0.00 | 0.00 | 1000.00 |
| 12,000+ - 22,900 | 1.71 | 0.00 | 0.00 | 60.00 |
| More than 22,900 | 5.04 | 0.00 | 0.00 | 300.00 |

**Table 2.3.4 In the past week about how much time, in minutes, have you spent using the artificial intelligence applications listed below, or similar such applications? CoPilot. Broken out by public or private college**

| Public or private college | Mean | Median | Minimum | Maximum |
|---|---|---|---|---|
| Public | 4.95 | 0.00 | 0.00 | 1000.00 |
| Private | 0.92 | 0.00 | 0.00 | 120.00 |

**Table 2.3.5 In the past week about how much time, in minutes, have you spent using the artificial intelligence applications listed below, or similar such applications? CoPilot. Broken out by age of respondent**

| Age of respondent | Mean | Median | Minimum | Maximum |
|---|---|---|---|---|
| Under 19 | 1.89 | 0.00 | 0.00 | 120.00 |
| 19-21 | 2.56 | 0.00 | 0.00 | 180.00 |
| 22-27 | 9.09 | 0.00 | 0.00 | 1000.00 |
| Over 28 | 4.48 | 0.00 | 0.00 | 200.00 |

**Table 2.3.6 In the past week about how much time, in minutes, have you spent using the artificial intelligence applications listed below, or similar such applications? CoPilot. Broken out by urban, suburban or rural upbringing**

| Urban, suburban or rural upbringing | Mean | Median | Minimum | Maximum |
|---|---|---|---|---|
| I grew up in a major city with more than 350,000 people | 9.78 | 0.00 | 0.00 | 1000.00 |
| I grew up in a small or medium sized city with less than 350,000 people. | 3.29 | 0.00 | 0.00 | 180.00 |
| I grew up in a suburban area | 1.49 | 0.00 | 0.00 | 180.00 |
| I grew up in a rural area. | 1.22 | 0.00 | 0.00 | 60.00 |
| Unknown | 0.00 | 0.00 | 0.00 | 0.00 |

**Table 2.3.7 In the past week about how much time, in minutes, have you spent using the artificial intelligence applications listed below, or similar such applications? CoPilot. Broken out by region of upbringing**

| Region of upbringing | Mean | Median | Minimum | Maximum |
|---|---|---|---|---|
| The South | 2.17 | 0.00 | 0.00 | 180.00 |
| The Northeast | 0.39 | 0.00 | 0.00 | 20.00 |
| The Midwest | 2.97 | 0.00 | 0.00 | 200.00 |
| The West | 1.95 | 0.00 | 0.00 | 180.00 |
| Abroad | 13.01 | 0.00 | 0.00 | 1000.00 |
| Unknown | 0.00 | 0.00 | 0.00 | 0.00 |

**Table 2.3.8 In the past week about how much time, in minutes, have you spent using the artificial intelligence applications listed below, or similar such applications? CoPilot. Broken out by year of class standing**

| Year of class standing | Mean | Median | Minimum | Maximum |
|---|---|---|---|---|
| First year student | 2.83 | 0.00 | 0.00 | 180.00 |
| Sophomore | 1.72 | 0.00 | 0.00 | 120.00 |
| Junior | 3.20 | 0.00 | 0.00 | 200.00 |
| Senior | 7.56 | 0.00 | 0.00 | 1000.00 |
| Unknown | 11.56 | 0.00 | 0.00 | 180.00 |

**Table 2.3.9 In the past week about how much time, in minutes, have you spent using the artificial intelligence applications listed below, or similar such applications? CoPilot. Broken out by annual family of origin income level**

| Annual family of origin income level | Mean | Median | Minimum | Maximum |
|---|---|---|---|---|
| Less than $50,000 per year | 7.72 | 0.00 | 0.00 | 1000.00 |
| $50,000 to $90,000 per year | 2.51 | 0.00 | 0.00 | 180.00 |
| $90,000+ to $150,000 per year | 2.33 | 0.00 | 0.00 | 180.00 |
| $150,000+ to $250,000 per year | 4.28 | 0.00 | 0.00 | 180.00 |
| More than $250,000 per year | 0.50 | 0.00 | 0.00 | 35.00 |
| Unknown | 0.00 | 0.00 | 0.00 | 0.00 |

**Table 2.3.10 In the past week about how much time, in minutes, have you spent using the artificial intelligence applications listed below, or similar such applications? CoPilot. Broken out by relationship with organized religion**

| Relationship with organized religion | Mean | Median | Minimum | Maximum |
|---|---|---|---|---|
| I practice a religion thoroughly and consider my religion to be a very important part of my life. | 3.94 | 0.00 | 0.00 | 180.00 |
| I practice a religion and try to attend regular services and to participate as much as I can. | 4.06 | 0.00 | 0.00 | 200.00 |
| I identify with a religion but can't say I put a lot of effort into practicing it. | 6.89 | 0.00 | 0.00 | 1000.00 |
| I don't really believe in or practice an organized religion. | 2.11 | 0.00 | 0.00 | 180.00 |
| Unknown | 0.00 | 0.00 | 0.00 | 0.00 |

**Table 2.3.11 In the past week about how much time, in minutes, have you spent using the artificial intelligence applications listed below, or similar such applications? CoPilot. Broken out by political views**

| Political views | Mean | Median | Minimum | Maximum |
|---|---|---|---|---|
| Very left wing | 2.91 | 0.00 | 0.00 | 180.00 |
| Liberal | 5.09 | 0.00 | 0.00 | 1000.00 |
| Middle of the road | 2.96 | 0.00 | 0.00 | 180.00 |
| Conservative | 4.82 | 0.00 | 0.00 | 200.00 |
| Very right wing | 7.00 | 0.00 | 0.00 | 120.00 |
| Unknown | 0.00 | 0.00 | 0.00 | 0.00 |

**Table 2.3.12 In the past week about how much time, in minutes, have you spent using the artificial intelligence applications listed below, or similar such applications? CoPilot. Broken out by college grades**

| College grades | Mean | Median | Minimum | Maximum |
|---|---|---|---|---|
| A or A- average or more | 4.28 | 0.00 | 0.00 | 1000.00 |
| B or B+ average | 3.31 | 0.00 | 0.00 | 180.00 |
| C or C+ or lower | 5.08 | 0.00 | 0.00 | 200.00 |
| Unknown | 0.00 | 0.00 | 0.00 | 0.00 |

### Table 2.3.13 In the past week about how much time, in minutes, have you spent using the artificial intelligence applications listed below, or similar such applications? CoPilot. Broken out by academic major

| Academic major | Mean | Median | Minimum | Maximum |
|---|---|---|---|---|
| Business, Economics or Finance | 1.71 | 0.00 | 0.00 | 60.00 |
| Psychology | 1.88 | 0.00 | 0.00 | 120.00 |
| Education or Library Science | 4.42 | 0.00 | 0.00 | 180.00 |
| Criminology/Law Enforcement | 2.00 | 0.00 | 0.00 | 30.00 |
| Occupational or Physical Therapy, Nursing, Public Health, Nutrition. other Health-Related | 4.35 | 0.00 | 0.00 | 300.00 |
| Communications, Media, Journalism | 5.42 | 0.00 | 0.00 | 120.00 |
| Fine Arts and Architecture | 0.24 | 0.00 | 0.00 | 15.00 |
| Music, Dance, Theater, other Performing Arts | 1.54 | 0.00 | 0.00 | 40.00 |
| English, Foreign Languages, Comp Literature, Creative Writing | 0.00 | 0.00 | 0.00 | 0.00 |
| Biology, Physics, Chemistry, Pre-Med | 9.29 | 0.00 | 0.00 | 1000.00 |
| Geology, Oceanography, Environmental Sciences | 0.00 | 0.00 | 0.00 | 0.00 |
| Engineering, Mathematics, Computer Science | 6.08 | 0.00 | 0.00 | 200.00 |
| History, Classics | 0.38 | 0.00 | 0.00 | 5.00 |
| Sociology, Political Science, Anthropology or other Social Science, except Economics and Psychology | 3.16 | 0.00 | 0.00 | 180.00 |
| Other | 0.00 | 0.00 | 0.00 | 0.00 |

**Table 2.3.14 In the past week about how much time, in minutes, have you spent using the artificial intelligence applications listed below, or similar such applications? CoPilot. Broken out by gender of respondent**

| Gender of respondent | Mean | Median | Minimum | Maximum |
|---|---|---|---|---|
| Male | 8.25 | 0.00 | 0.00 | 1000.00 |
| Female | 2.06 | 0.00 | 0.00 | 180.00 |
| Transgender | 0.26 | 0.00 | 0.00 | 15.00 |
| Unknown | 0.00 | 0.00 | 0.00 | 0.00 |

**Table 2.3.15 In the past week about how much time, in minutes, have you spent using the artificial intelligence applications listed below, or similar such applications? CoPilot. Broken out by status of current residency**

| Status of current residency | Mean | Median | Minimum | Maximum |
|---|---|---|---|---|
| At home with my parents or guardian | 2.26 | 0.00 | 0.00 | 180.00 |
| Off campus with others who are not my parents or guardian | 4.13 | 0.00 | 0.00 | 300.00 |
| Off campus alone | 15.61 | 0.00 | 0.00 | 1000.00 |
| On campus in the dorms or college-provided suites | 1.80 | 0.00 | 0.00 | 120.00 |
| Unknown | 0.00 | 0.00 | 0.00 | 0.00 |

**Table 2.3.16 In the past week about how much time, in minutes, have you spent using the artificial intelligence applications listed below, or similar such applications? CoPilot. Broken out by current employment situation**

| Current employment situation | Mean | Median | Minimum | Maximum |
|---|---|---|---|---|
| I don't have a full or part time job. | 5.61 | 0.00 | 0.00 | 1000.00 |
| I have a part time job. | 2.64 | 0.00 | 0.00 | 300.00 |
| I have a full time job. | 3.95 | 0.00 | 0.00 | 120.00 |
| Unknown | 0.00 | 0.00 | 0.00 | 0.00 |

**Table 2.3.17 In the past week about how much time, in minutes, have you spent using the artificial intelligence applications listed below, or similar such applications? CoPilot. Broken out by sexual orientation**

| Sexual orientation | Mean | Median | Minimum | Maximum |
|---|---|---|---|---|
| Heterosexual or "straight" | 4.81 | 0.00 | 0.00 | 1000.00 |
| Homosexual or "gay" | 2.23 | 0.00 | 0.00 | 60.00 |
| Bi-sexual | 2.25 | 0.00 | 0.00 | 180.00 |
| Unknown | 0.67 | 0.00 | 0.00 | 10.00 |

**Table 2.3.18 In the past week about how much time, in minutes, have you spent using the artificial intelligence applications listed below, or similar such applications? CoPilot. Broken out by SAT or ACT score**

| SAT or ACT score | Mean | Median | Minimum | Maximum |
|---|---|---|---|---|
| 30 or over ACT or 1350 or over SAT | 1.63 | 0.00 | 0.00 | 120.00 |
| 24-29 ACT or 1170 to 1349 SAT | 2.51 | 0.00 | 0.00 | 120.00 |
| 20-23 ACT or 1050 to 1169 SAT | 1.61 | 0.00 | 0.00 | 180.00 |
| 17-19 ACT or 900 to 1050 SAT | 5.05 | 0.00 | 0.00 | 180.00 |
| 16 or Under ACT or Under 900 SAT | 0.74 | 0.00 | 0.00 | 15.00 |
| Never took either test | 11.08 | 0.00 | 0.00 | 1000.00 |
| Unknown | 0.00 | 0.00 | 0.00 | 0.00 |

**Table 2.3.19 In the past week about how much time, in minutes, have you spent using the artificial intelligence applications listed below, or similar such applications? CoPilot. Broken out by race or ethnicity**

| Race or ethnicity | Mean | Median | Minimum | Maximum |
|---|---|---|---|---|
| White or Caucasian | 1.77 | 0.00 | 0.00 | 180.00 |
| Black or African American | 5.14 | 0.00 | 0.00 | 200.00 |
| Latino or Hispanic | 3.05 | 0.00 | 0.00 | 120.00 |
| Asian or Asian American | 11.57 | 0.00 | 0.00 | 1000.00 |
| American Indigenous, Eskimo, Pacific Islander, Hawaiian Native | 0.00 | 0.00 | 0.00 | 0.00 |
| Mixed race | 1.69 | 0.00 | 0.00 | 60.00 |
| Unknown | 1.25 | 0.00 | 0.00 | 15.00 |

**Table 2.3.20 In the past week about how much time, in minutes, have you spent using the artificial intelligence applications listed below, or similar such applications? CoPilot. Broken out by religion**

| Religion | Mean | Median | Minimum | Maximum |
|---|---|---|---|---|
| I do not practice or identify with an organized religion | 1.42 | 0.00 | 0.00 | 180.00 |
| Hinduism | 24.40 | 0.00 | 0.00 | 1000.00 |
| Islam | 5.52 | 0.00 | 0.00 | 120.00 |
| Judaism | 0.07 | 0.00 | 0.00 | 2.00 |
| Mormon | 5.00 | 0.00 | 0.00 | 30.00 |
| Catholic | 3.74 | 0.00 | 0.00 | 90.00 |
| Lutheran | 0.47 | 0.00 | 0.00 | 15.00 |
| Baptist | 0.59 | 0.00 | 0.00 | 30.00 |
| Evangelical Protestant Christianity | 5.22 | 0.00 | 0.00 | 120.00 |
| Protestant Christianity | 4.80 | 0.00 | 0.00 | 200.00 |
| Orthodox Christianity | 0.00 | 0.00 | 0.00 | 0.00 |
| Buddhism | 1.75 | 0.00 | 0.00 | 20.00 |
| Non-Denominational Christianity | 4.55 | 0.00 | 0.00 | 180.00 |
| Other | 10.29 | 0.00 | 0.00 | 300.00 |

**Table 2.4.1 In the past week about how much time, in minutes, have you spent using the artificial intelligence applications listed below, or similar such applications? Midjourney.**

| | Mean | Median | Minimum | Maximum |
|---|---|---|---|---|
| Entire sample | 0.47 | 0.00 | 0.00 | 300.00 |

Table 2.4.2 In the past week about how much time, in minutes, have you spent using the artificial intelligence applications listed below, or similar such applications? Midjourney. Broken out by tuition of college attended

| Tuition of college attended | Mean | Median | Minimum | Maximum |
|---|---|---|---|---|
| Less than $6,000 | 0.11 | 0.00 | 0.00 | 30.00 |
| $6,000+ - $12,000 | 1.73 | 0.00 | 0.00 | 300.00 |
| $12,000+ - $20,000 | 0.06 | 0.00 | 0.00 | 10.00 |
| More than $20,000 | 0.04 | 0.00 | 0.00 | 10.00 |

Table 2.4.3 In the past week about how much time, in minutes, have you spent using the artificial intelligence applications listed below, or similar such applications? Midjourney. Broken out by enrollment of college attended

| Enrollment of college attended | Mean | Median | Minimum | Maximum |
|---|---|---|---|---|
| Less than 5,000 | 0.04 | 0.00 | 0.00 | 10.00 |
| 5,000+ - 12,000 | 0.46 | 0.00 | 0.00 | 120.00 |
| 12,000+ - 22,900 | 1.37 | 0.00 | 0.00 | 300.00 |
| More than 22,900 | 0.11 | 0.00 | 0.00 | 30.00 |

Table 2.4.4 In the past week about how much time, in minutes, have you spent using the artificial intelligence applications listed below, or similar such applications? Midjourney. Broken out by public or private college

| Public or private college | Mean | Median | Minimum | Maximum |
|---|---|---|---|---|
| Public | 0.60 | 0.00 | 0.00 | 300.00 |
| Private | 0.04 | 0.00 | 0.00 | 10.00 |

**Table 2.4.5 In the past week about how much time, in minutes, have you spent using the artificial intelligence applications listed below, or similar such applications? Midjourney. Broken out by age of respondent**

| Age of respondent | Mean | Median | Minimum | Maximum |
|---|---|---|---|---|
| Under 19 | 0.79 | 0.00 | 0.00 | 300.00 |
| 19-21 | 0.04 | 0.00 | 0.00 | 10.00 |
| 22-27 | 0.62 | 0.00 | 0.00 | 120.00 |
| Over 28 | 0.21 | 0.00 | 0.00 | 30.00 |

**Table 2.4.6 In the past week about how much time, in minutes, have you spent using the artificial intelligence applications listed below, or similar such applications? Midjourney. Broken out by urban, suburban or rural upbringing**

| Urban, suburban or rural upbringing | Mean | Median | Minimum | Maximum |
|---|---|---|---|---|
| I grew up in a major city with more than 350,000 people | 1.76 | 0.00 | 0.00 | 300.00 |
| I grew up in a small or medium sized city with less than 350,000 people. | 0.04 | 0.00 | 0.00 | 10.00 |
| I grew up in a suburban area | 0.00 | 0.00 | 0.00 | 0.00 |
| I grew up in a rural area. | 0.03 | 0.00 | 0.00 | 5.00 |
| Unknown | 0.00 | 0.00 | 0.00 | 0.00 |

**Table 2.4.7 In the past week about how much time, in minutes, have you spent using the artificial intelligence applications listed below, or similar such applications? Midjourney. Broken out by region of upbringing**

| Region of upbringing | Mean | Median | Minimum | Maximum |
|---|---|---|---|---|
| The South | 0.49 | 0.00 | 0.00 | 120.00 |
| The Northeast | 0.00 | 0.00 | 0.00 | 0.00 |
| The Midwest | 0.79 | 0.00 | 0.00 | 300.00 |
| The West | 0.00 | 0.00 | 0.00 | 0.00 |
| Abroad | 0.27 | 0.00 | 0.00 | 30.00 |
| Unknown | 0.00 | 0.00 | 0.00 | 0.00 |

**Table 2.4.8 In the past week about how much time, in minutes, have you spent using the artificial intelligence applications listed below, or similar such applications? Midjourney. Broken out by year of class standing**

| Year of class standing | Mean | Median | Minimum | Maximum |
|---|---|---|---|---|
| First year student | 0.00 | 0.00 | 0.00 | 0.00 |
| Sophomore | 1.72 | 0.00 | 0.00 | 300.00 |
| Junior | 0.06 | 0.00 | 0.00 | 10.00 |
| Senior | 0.62 | 0.00 | 0.00 | 120.00 |
| Unknown | 0.00 | 0.00 | 0.00 | 0.00 |

**Table 2.4.9 In the past week about how much time, in minutes, have you spent using the artificial intelligence applications listed below, or similar such applications? Midjourney. Broken out by annual family of origin income level**

| Annual family of origin income level | Mean | Median | Minimum | Maximum |
|---|---|---|---|---|
| Less than $50,000 per year | 0.14 | 0.00 | 0.00 | 30.00 |
| $50,000 to $90,000 per year | 0.02 | 0.00 | 0.00 | 5.00 |
| $90,000+ to $150,000 per year | 0.00 | 0.00 | 0.00 | 0.00 |
| $150,000+ to $250,000 per year | 4.04 | 0.00 | 0.00 | 300.00 |
| More than $250,000 per year | 0.11 | 0.00 | 0.00 | 10.00 |
| Unknown | 0.00 | 0.00 | 0.00 | 0.00 |

**Table 2.4.10 In the past week about how much time, in minutes, have you spent using the artificial intelligence applications listed below, or similar such applications? Midjourney. Broken out by relationship with organized religion**

| Relationship with organized religion | Mean | Median | Minimum | Maximum |
|---|---|---|---|---|
| I practice a religion thoroughly and consider my religion to be a very important part of my life. | 0.03 | 0.00 | 0.00 | 5.00 |
| I practice a religion and try to attend regular services and to participate as much as I can. | 0.19 | 0.00 | 0.00 | 30.00 |
| I identify with a religion but can't say I put a lot of effort into practicing it. | 1.13 | 0.00 | 0.00 | 300.00 |
| I don't really believe in or practice an organized religion. | 0.35 | 0.00 | 0.00 | 120.00 |
| Unknown | 0.00 | 0.00 | 0.00 | 0.00 |

**Table 2.4.11 In the past week about how much time, in minutes, have you spent using the artificial intelligence applications listed below, or similar such applications? Midjourney. Broken out by political views**

| Political views | Mean | Median | Minimum | Maximum |
|---|---|---|---|---|
| Very left wing | 0.00 | 0.00 | 0.00 | 0.00 |
| Liberal | 0.35 | 0.00 | 0.00 | 120.00 |
| Middle of the road | 1.03 | 0.00 | 0.00 | 300.00 |
| Conservative | 0.04 | 0.00 | 0.00 | 5.00 |
| Very right wing | 0.00 | 0.00 | 0.00 | 0.00 |
| Unknown | 0.00 | 0.00 | 0.00 | 0.00 |

**Table 2.4.12 In the past week about how much time, in minutes, have you spent using the artificial intelligence applications listed below, or similar such applications? Midjourney. Broken out by college grades**

| College grades | Mean | Median | Minimum | Maximum |
|---|---|---|---|---|
| A or A- average or more | 0.70 | 0.00 | 0.00 | 300.00 |
| B or B+ average | 0.07 | 0.00 | 0.00 | 10.00 |
| C or C+ or lower | 0.00 | 0.00 | 0.00 | 0.00 |
| Unknown | 0.00 | 0.00 | 0.00 | 0.00 |

**Table 2.4.13 In the past week about how much time, in minutes, have you spent using the artificial intelligence applications listed below, or similar such applications? Midjourney. Broken out by academic major**

| Academic major | Mean | Median | Minimum | Maximum |
|---|---|---|---|---|
| Business, Economics or Finance | 0.00 | 0.00 | 0.00 | 0.00 |
| Psychology | 0.00 | 0.00 | 0.00 | 0.00 |
| Education or Library Science | 0.00 | 0.00 | 0.00 | 0.00 |
| Criminology/Law Enforcement | 0.00 | 0.00 | 0.00 | 0.00 |
| Occupational or Physical Therapy, Nursing, Public Health, Nutrition. other Health-Related | 0.00 | 0.00 | 0.00 | 0.00 |
| Communications, Media, Journalism | 0.00 | 0.00 | 0.00 | 0.00 |
| Fine Arts and Architecture | 4.84 | 0.00 | 0.00 | 300.00 |
| Music, Dance, Theater, other Performing Arts | 0.00 | 0.00 | 0.00 | 0.00 |
| English, Foreign Languages, Comp Literature, Creative Writing | 0.00 | 0.00 | 0.00 | 0.00 |
| Biology, Physics, Chemistry, Pre-Med | 0.00 | 0.00 | 0.00 | 0.00 |
| Geology, Oceanography, Environmental Sciences | 0.00 | 0.00 | 0.00 | 0.00 |
| Engineering, Mathematics, Computer Science | 0.87 | 0.00 | 0.00 | 120.00 |
| History, Classics | 0.00 | 0.00 | 0.00 | 0.00 |
| Sociology, Political Science, Anthropology or other Social Science, except Economics and Psychology | 0.00 | 0.00 | 0.00 | 0.00 |
| Other | 0.00 | 0.00 | 0.00 | 0.00 |

**Table 2.4.14 In the past week about how much time, in minutes, have you spent using the artificial intelligence applications listed below, or similar such applications? Midjourney. Broken out by gender of respondent**

| Gender of respondent | Mean | Median | Minimum | Maximum |
|---|---|---|---|---|
| Male | 0.45 | 0.00 | 0.00 | 120.00 |
| Female | 0.52 | 0.00 | 0.00 | 300.00 |
| Transgender | 0.00 | 0.00 | 0.00 | 0.00 |
| Unknown | 0.00 | 0.00 | 0.00 | 0.00 |

**Table 2.4.15 In the past week about how much time, in minutes, have you spent using the artificial intelligence applications listed below, or similar such applications? Midjourney. Broken out by status of current residency**

| Status of current residency | Mean | Median | Minimum | Maximum |
|---|---|---|---|---|
| At home with my parents or guardian | 0.02 | 0.00 | 0.00 | 5.00 |
| Off campus with others who are not my parents or guardian | 1.31 | 0.00 | 0.00 | 300.00 |
| Off campus alone | 1.13 | 0.00 | 0.00 | 120.00 |
| On campus in the dorms or college-provided suites | 0.03 | 0.00 | 0.00 | 10.00 |
| Unknown | 0.00 | 0.00 | 0.00 | 0.00 |

**Table 2.4.16 In the past week about how much time, in minutes, have you spent using the artificial intelligence applications listed below, or similar such applications? Midjourney. Broken out by current employment situation**

| Current employment situation | Mean | Median | Minimum | Maximum |
|---|---|---|---|---|
| I don't have a full or part time job. | 0.33 | 0.00 | 0.00 | 120.00 |
| I have a part time job. | 0.70 | 0.00 | 0.00 | 300.00 |
| I have a full time job. | 0.20 | 0.00 | 0.00 | 30.00 |
| Unknown | 0.00 | 0.00 | 0.00 | 0.00 |

**Table 2.4.17 In the past week about how much time, in minutes, have you spent using the artificial intelligence applications listed below, or similar such applications? Midjourney. Broken out by sexual orientation**

| Sexual orientation | Mean | Median | Minimum | Maximum |
|---|---|---|---|---|
| Heterosexual or "straight" | 0.67 | 0.00 | 0.00 | 300.00 |
| Homosexual or "gay" | 0.00 | 0.00 | 0.00 | 0.00 |
| Bi-sexual | 0.00 | 0.00 | 0.00 | 0.00 |
| Unknown | 0.00 | 0.00 | 0.00 | 0.00 |

**Table 2.4.18 In the past week about how much time, in minutes, have you spent using the artificial intelligence applications listed below, or similar such applications? Midjourney. Broken out by SAT or ACT score**

| SAT or ACT score | Mean | Median | Minimum | Maximum |
|---|---|---|---|---|
| 30 or over ACT or 1350 or over SAT | 0.08 | 0.00 | 0.00 | 10.00 |
| 24-29 ACT or 1170 to 1349 SAT | 1.21 | 0.00 | 0.00 | 300.00 |
| 20-23 ACT or 1050 to 1169 SAT | 0.67 | 0.00 | 0.00 | 120.00 |
| 17-19 ACT or 900 to 1050 SAT | 0.00 | 0.00 | 0.00 | 0.00 |
| 16 or Under ACT or Under 900 SAT | 0.00 | 0.00 | 0.00 | 0.00 |
| Never took either test | 0.14 | 0.00 | 0.00 | 30.00 |
| Unknown | 0.00 | 0.00 | 0.00 | 0.00 |

**Table 2.4.19 In the past week about how much time, in minutes, have you spent using the artificial intelligence applications listed below, or similar such applications? Midjourney. Broken out by race or ethnicity**

| Race or ethnicity | Mean | Median | Minimum | Maximum |
|---|---|---|---|---|
| White or Caucasian | 0.61 | 0.00 | 0.00 | 300.00 |
| Black or African American | 0.23 | 0.00 | 0.00 | 30.00 |
| Latino or Hispanic | 0.00 | 0.00 | 0.00 | 0.00 |
| Asian or Asian American | 0.76 | 0.00 | 0.00 | 120.00 |
| American Indigenous, Eskimo, Pacific Islander, Hawaiian Native | 0.00 | 0.00 | 0.00 | 0.00 |
| Mixed race | 0.00 | 0.00 | 0.00 | 0.00 |
| Unknown | 0.00 | 0.00 | 0.00 | 0.00 |

**Table 2.4.20 In the past week about how much time, in minutes, have you spent using the artificial intelligence applications listed below, or similar such applications? Midjourney. Broken out by religion**

| Religion | Mean | Median | Minimum | Maximum |
|---|---|---|---|---|
| I do not practice or identify with an organized religion | 0.83 | 0.00 | 0.00 | 300.00 |
| Hinduism | 0.20 | 0.00 | 0.00 | 10.00 |
| Islam | 0.00 | 0.00 | 0.00 | 0.00 |
| Judaism | 0.00 | 0.00 | 0.00 | 0.00 |
| Mormon | 0.00 | 0.00 | 0.00 | 0.00 |
| Catholic | 0.22 | 0.00 | 0.00 | 30.00 |
| Lutheran | 0.16 | 0.00 | 0.00 | 5.00 |
| Baptist | 0.00 | 0.00 | 0.00 | 0.00 |
| Evangelical Protestant Christianity | 0.00 | 0.00 | 0.00 | 0.00 |
| Protestant Christianity | 0.00 | 0.00 | 0.00 | 0.00 |
| Orthodox Christianity | 0.00 | 0.00 | 0.00 | 0.00 |
| Buddhism | 0.00 | 0.00 | 0.00 | 0.00 |
| Non-Denominational Christianity | 1.08 | 0.00 | 0.00 | 120.00 |
| Other | 0.00 | 0.00 | 0.00 | 0.00 |

**Table 2.5.1 In the past week about how much time, in minutes, have you spent using the artificial intelligence applications listed below, or similar such applications? Claude.**

| | Mean | Median | Minimum | Maximum |
|---|---|---|---|---|
| Entire sample | 1.29 | 0.00 | 0.00 | 300.00 |

**Table 2.5.2 In the past week about how much time, in minutes, have you spent using the artificial intelligence applications listed below, or similar such applications? Claude. Broken out by tuition of college attended**

| Tuition of college attended | Mean | Median | Minimum | Maximum |
|---|---|---|---|---|
| Less than $6,000 | 0.37 | 0.00 | 0.00 | 40.00 |
| $6,000+ - $12,000 | 2.28 | 0.00 | 0.00 | 300.00 |
| $12,000+ - $20,000 | 1.56 | 0.00 | 0.00 | 120.00 |
| More than $20,000 | 0.99 | 0.00 | 0.00 | 60.00 |

**Table 2.5.3 In the past week about how much time, in minutes, have you spent using the artificial intelligence applications listed below, or similar such applications? Claude. Broken out by enrollment of college attended**

| Enrollment of college attended | Mean | Median | Minimum | Maximum |
|---|---|---|---|---|
| Less than 5,000 | 0.97 | 0.00 | 0.00 | 60.00 |
| 5,000+ - 12,000 | 2.21 | 0.00 | 0.00 | 300.00 |
| 12,000+ - 22,900 | 1.69 | 0.00 | 0.00 | 120.00 |
| More than 22,900 | 0.36 | 0.00 | 0.00 | 40.00 |

**Table 2.5.4 In the past week about how much time, in minutes, have you spent using the artificial intelligence applications listed below, or similar such applications? Claude. Broken out by public or private college**

| Public or private college | Mean | Median | Minimum | Maximum |
|---|---|---|---|---|
| Public | 1.36 | 0.00 | 0.00 | 300.00 |
| Private | 1.05 | 0.00 | 0.00 | 60.00 |

Table 2.5.5 In the past week about how much time, in minutes, have you spent using the artificial intelligence applications listed below, or similar such applications? Claude. Broken out by age of respondent

| Age of respondent | Mean | Median | Minimum | Maximum |
|---|---|---|---|---|
| Under 19 | 0.42 | 0.00 | 0.00 | 60.00 |
| 19-21 | 1.03 | 0.00 | 0.00 | 120.00 |
| 22-27 | 2.99 | 0.00 | 0.00 | 300.00 |
| Over 28 | 1.44 | 0.00 | 0.00 | 120.00 |

Table 2.5.6 In the past week about how much time, in minutes, have you spent using the artificial intelligence applications listed below, or similar such applications? Claude. Broken out by urban, suburban or rural upbringing

| Urban, suburban or rural upbringing | Mean | Median | Minimum | Maximum |
|---|---|---|---|---|
| I grew up in a major city with more than 350,000 people | 2.56 | 0.00 | 0.00 | 240.00 |
| I grew up in a small or medium sized city with less than 350,000 people. | 0.22 | 0.00 | 0.00 | 15.00 |
| I grew up in a suburban area | 1.31 | 0.00 | 0.00 | 300.00 |
| I grew up in a rural area. | 0.94 | 0.00 | 0.00 | 120.00 |
| Unknown | 0.00 | 0.00 | 0.00 | 0.00 |

**Table 2.5.7 In the past week about how much time, in minutes, have you spent using the artificial intelligence applications listed below, or similar such applications? Claude. Broken out by region of upbringing**

| Region of upbringing | Mean | Median | Minimum | Maximum |
|---|---|---|---|---|
| The South | 1.96 | 0.00 | 0.00 | 240.00 |
| The Northeast | 0.22 | 0.00 | 0.00 | 10.00 |
| The Midwest | 0.21 | 0.00 | 0.00 | 40.00 |
| The West | 0.55 | 0.00 | 0.00 | 30.00 |
| Abroad | 4.05 | 0.00 | 0.00 | 300.00 |
| Unknown | 0.00 | 0.00 | 0.00 | 0.00 |

**Table 2.5.8 In the past week about how much time, in minutes, have you spent using the artificial intelligence applications listed below, or similar such applications? Claude. Broken out by year of class standing**

| Year of class standing | Mean | Median | Minimum | Maximum |
|---|---|---|---|---|
| First year student | 0.79 | 0.00 | 0.00 | 120.00 |
| Sophomore | 0.33 | 0.00 | 0.00 | 20.00 |
| Junior | 0.88 | 0.00 | 0.00 | 60.00 |
| Senior | 3.04 | 0.00 | 0.00 | 300.00 |
| Unknown | 0.31 | 0.00 | 0.00 | 5.00 |

**Table 2.5.9 In the past week about how much time, in minutes, have you spent using the artificial intelligence applications listed below, or similar such applications? Claude. Broken out by annual family of origin income level**

| Annual family of origin income level | Mean | Median | Minimum | Maximum |
|---|---|---|---|---|
| Less than $50,000 per year | 0.68 | 0.00 | 0.00 | 120.00 |
| $50,000 to $90,000 per year | 1.67 | 0.00 | 0.00 | 300.00 |
| $90,000+ to $150,000 per year | 0.68 | 0.00 | 0.00 | 60.00 |
| $150,000+ to $250,000 per year | 3.89 | 0.00 | 0.00 | 240.00 |
| More than $250,000 per year | 0.78 | 0.00 | 0.00 | 30.00 |
| Unknown | 0.00 | 0.00 | 0.00 | 0.00 |

**Table 2.5.10 In the past week about how much time, in minutes, have you spent using the artificial intelligence applications listed below, or similar such applications? Claude. Broken out by relationship with organized religion**

| Relationship with organized religion | Mean | Median | Minimum | Maximum |
|---|---|---|---|---|
| I practice a religion thoroughly and consider my religion to be a very important part of my life. | 1.66 | 0.00 | 0.00 | 300.00 |
| I practice a religion and try to attend regular services and to participate as much as I can. | 1.27 | 0.00 | 0.00 | 120.00 |
| I identify with a religion but can't say I put a lot of effort into practicing it. | 0.82 | 0.00 | 0.00 | 60.00 |
| I don't really believe in or practice an organized religion. | 1.46 | 0.00 | 0.00 | 240.00 |
| Unknown | 0.00 | 0.00 | 0.00 | 0.00 |

**Table 2.5.11 In the past week about how much time, in minutes, have you spent using the artificial intelligence applications listed below, or similar such applications? Claude. Broken out by political views**

| Political views | Mean | Median | Minimum | Maximum |
|---|---|---|---|---|
| Very left wing | 1.26 | 0.00 | 0.00 | 120.00 |
| Liberal | 1.02 | 0.00 | 0.00 | 240.00 |
| Middle of the road | 2.19 | 0.00 | 0.00 | 300.00 |
| Conservative | 0.11 | 0.00 | 0.00 | 15.00 |
| Very right wing | 0.00 | 0.00 | 0.00 | 0.00 |
| Unknown | 0.00 | 0.00 | 0.00 | 0.00 |

**Table 2.5.12 In the past week about how much time, in minutes, have you spent using the artificial intelligence applications listed below, or similar such applications? Claude. Broken out by college grades**

| College grades | Mean | Median | Minimum | Maximum |
|---|---|---|---|---|
| A or A- average or more | 1.36 | 0.00 | 0.00 | 240.00 |
| B or B+ average | 1.41 | 0.00 | 0.00 | 300.00 |
| C or C+ or lower | 0.00 | 0.00 | 0.00 | 0.00 |
| Unknown | 0.00 | 0.00 | 0.00 | 0.00 |

**Table 2.5.13 In the past week about how much time, in minutes, have you spent using the artificial intelligence applications listed below, or similar such applications? Claude. Broken out by academic major**

| Academic major | Mean | Median | Minimum | Maximum |
|---|---|---|---|---|
| Business, Economics or Finance | 0.91 | 0.00 | 0.00 | 60.00 |
| Psychology | 0.43 | 0.00 | 0.00 | 40.00 |
| Education or Library Science | 0.20 | 0.00 | 0.00 | 15.00 |
| Criminology/Law Enforcement | 0.00 | 0.00 | 0.00 | 0.00 |
| Occupational or Physical Therapy, Nursing, Public Health, Nutrition. other Health-Related | 0.00 | 0.00 | 0.00 | 0.00 |
| Communications, Media, Journalism | 0.00 | 0.00 | 0.00 | 0.00 |
| Fine Arts and Architecture | 0.00 | 0.00 | 0.00 | 0.00 |
| Music, Dance, Theater, other Performing Arts | 0.00 | 0.00 | 0.00 | 0.00 |
| English, Foreign Languages, Comp Literature, Creative Writing | 0.00 | 0.00 | 0.00 | 0.00 |
| Biology, Physics, Chemistry, Pre-Med | 0.41 | 0.00 | 0.00 | 20.00 |
| Geology, Oceanography, Environmental Sciences | 0.00 | 0.00 | 0.00 | 0.00 |
| Engineering, Mathematics, Computer Science | 4.36 | 0.00 | 0.00 | 300.00 |
| History, Classics | 4.62 | 0.00 | 0.00 | 60.00 |
| Sociology, Political Science, Anthropology or other Social Science, except Economics and Psychology | 1.97 | 0.00 | 0.00 | 120.00 |
| Other | 0.00 | 0.00 | 0.00 | 0.00 |

**Table 2.5.14 In the past week about how much time, in minutes, have you spent using the artificial intelligence applications listed below, or similar such applications? Claude. Broken out by gender of respondent**

| Gender of respondent | Mean | Median | Minimum | Maximum |
|---|---|---|---|---|
| Male | 2.76 | 0.00 | 0.00 | 300.00 |
| Female | 0.60 | 0.00 | 0.00 | 120.00 |
| Transgender | 0.00 | 0.00 | 0.00 | 0.00 |
| Unknown | 0.00 | 0.00 | 0.00 | 0.00 |

**Table 2.5.15 In the past week about how much time, in minutes, have you spent using the artificial intelligence applications listed below, or similar such applications? Claude. Broken out by status of current residency**

| Status of current residency | Mean | Median | Minimum | Maximum |
|---|---|---|---|---|
| At home with my parents or guardian | 0.36 | 0.00 | 0.00 | 60.00 |
| Off campus with others who are not my parents or guardian | 2.14 | 0.00 | 0.00 | 300.00 |
| Off campus alone | 2.35 | 0.00 | 0.00 | 240.00 |
| On campus in the dorms or college-provided suites | 0.99 | 0.00 | 0.00 | 120.00 |
| Unknown | 0.00 | 0.00 | 0.00 | 0.00 |

**Table 2.5.16 In the past week about how much time, in minutes, have you spent using the artificial intelligence applications listed below, or similar such applications? Claude. Broken out by current employment situation**

| Current employment situation | Mean | Median | Minimum | Maximum |
|---|---|---|---|---|
| I don't have a full or part time job. | 2.37 | 0.00 | 0.00 | 300.00 |
| I have a part time job. | 0.68 | 0.00 | 0.00 | 120.00 |
| I have a full time job. | 0.20 | 0.00 | 0.00 | 30.00 |
| Unknown | 0.00 | 0.00 | 0.00 | 0.00 |

**Table 2.5.17 In the past week about how much time, in minutes, have you spent using the artificial intelligence applications listed below, or similar such applications? Claude. Broken out by sexual orientation**

| Sexual orientation | Mean | Median | Minimum | Maximum |
|---|---|---|---|---|
| Heterosexual or "straight" | 1.52 | 0.00 | 0.00 | 300.00 |
| Homosexual or "gay" | 0.07 | 0.00 | 0.00 | 5.00 |
| Bi-sexual | 0.89 | 0.00 | 0.00 | 120.00 |
| Unknown | 2.00 | 0.00 | 0.00 | 20.00 |

**Table 2.5.18 In the past week about how much time, in minutes, have you spent using the artificial intelligence applications listed below, or similar such applications? Claude. Broken out by SAT or ACT score**

| SAT or ACT score | Mean | Median | Minimum | Maximum |
|---|---|---|---|---|
| 30 or over ACT or 1350 or over SAT | 1.69 | 0.00 | 0.00 | 120.00 |
| 24-29 ACT or 1170 to 1349 SAT | 0.76 | 0.00 | 0.00 | 120.00 |
| 20-23 ACT or 1050 to 1169 SAT | 1.67 | 0.00 | 0.00 | 240.00 |
| 17-19 ACT or 900 to 1050 SAT | 0.00 | 0.00 | 0.00 | 0.00 |
| 16 or Under ACT or Under 900 SAT | 0.00 | 0.00 | 0.00 | 0.00 |
| Never took either test | 1.90 | 0.00 | 0.00 | 300.00 |
| Unknown | 0.00 | 0.00 | 0.00 | 0.00 |

**Table 2.5.19 In the past week about how much time, in minutes, have you spent using the artificial intelligence applications listed below, or similar such applications? Claude. Broken out by race or ethnicity**

| Race or ethnicity | Mean | Median | Minimum | Maximum |
|---|---|---|---|---|
| White or Caucasian | 0.35 | 0.00 | 0.00 | 40.00 |
| Black or African American | 0.60 | 0.00 | 0.00 | 30.00 |
| Latino or Hispanic | 0.05 | 0.00 | 0.00 | 5.00 |
| Asian or Asian American | 5.17 | 0.00 | 0.00 | 300.00 |
| American Indigenous, Eskimo, Pacific Islander, Hawaiian Native | 0.00 | 0.00 | 0.00 | 0.00 |
| Mixed race | 1.83 | 0.00 | 0.00 | 120.00 |
| Unknown | 0.00 | 0.00 | 0.00 | 0.00 |

**Table 2.5.20 In the past week about how much time, in minutes, have you spent using the artificial intelligence applications listed below, or similar such applications? Claude. Broken out by religion**

| Religion | Mean | Median | Minimum | Maximum |
|---|---|---|---|---|
| I do not practice or identify with an organized religion | 1.64 | 0.00 | 0.00 | 300.00 |
| Hinduism | 1.40 | 0.00 | 0.00 | 60.00 |
| Islam | 3.33 | 0.00 | 0.00 | 120.00 |
| Judaism | 0.00 | 0.00 | 0.00 | 0.00 |
| Mormon | 0.00 | 0.00 | 0.00 | 0.00 |
| Catholic | 0.22 | 0.00 | 0.00 | 30.00 |
| Lutheran | 2.81 | 0.00 | 0.00 | 60.00 |
| Baptist | 0.00 | 0.00 | 0.00 | 0.00 |
| Evangelical Protestant Christianity | 0.87 | 0.00 | 0.00 | 15.00 |
| Protestant Christianity | 0.00 | 0.00 | 0.00 | 0.00 |
| Orthodox Christianity | 1.11 | 0.00 | 0.00 | 20.00 |
| Buddhism | 0.00 | 0.00 | 0.00 | 0.00 |
| Non-Denominational Christianity | 2.16 | 0.00 | 0.00 | 240.00 |
| Other | 1.03 | 0.00 | 0.00 | 60.00 |

**Table 2.6.1 In the past week about how much time, in minutes, have you spent using the artificial intelligence applications listed below, or similar such applications? All Other AI Generative Applications.**

| | Mean | Median | Minimum | Maximum |
|---|---|---|---|---|
| Entire sample | 3.23 | 0.00 | 0.00 | 500.00 |

**Table 2.6.2 In the past week about how much time, in minutes, have you spent using the artificial intelligence applications listed below, or similar such applications? All Other AI Generative Applications. Broken out by tuition of college attended**

| Tuition of college attended | Mean | Median | Minimum | Maximum |
|---|---|---|---|---|
| Less than $6,000 | 2.86 | 0.00 | 0.00 | 180.00 |
| $6,000+ - $12,000 | 6.16 | 0.00 | 0.00 | 500.00 |
| $12,000+ - $20,000 | 3.44 | 0.00 | 0.00 | 200.00 |
| More than $20,000 | 0.51 | 0.00 | 0.00 | 60.00 |

**Table 2.6.3 In the past week about how much time, in minutes, have you spent using the artificial intelligence applications listed below, or similar such applications? All Other AI Generative Applications. Broken out by enrollment of college attended**

| Enrollment of college attended | Mean | Median | Minimum | Maximum |
|---|---|---|---|---|
| Less than 5,000 | 0.50 | 0.00 | 0.00 | 60.00 |
| 5,000+ - 12,000 | 2.95 | 0.00 | 0.00 | 240.00 |
| 12,000+ - 22,900 | 6.84 | 0.00 | 0.00 | 500.00 |
| More than 22,900 | 2.95 | 0.00 | 0.00 | 180.00 |

**Table 2.6.4 In the past week about how much time, in minutes, have you spent using the artificial intelligence applications listed below, or similar such applications? All Other AI Generative Applications. Broken out by public or private college**

| Public or private college | Mean | Median | Minimum | Maximum |
|---|---|---|---|---|
| Public | 4.04 | 0.00 | 0.00 | 500.00 |
| Private | 0.53 | 0.00 | 0.00 | 60.00 |

**Table 2.6.5 In the past week about how much time, in minutes, have you spent using the artificial intelligence applications listed below, or similar such applications? All Other AI Generative Applications. Broken out by age of respondent**

| Age of respondent | Mean | Median | Minimum | Maximum |
|---|---|---|---|---|
| Under 19 | 2.84 | 0.00 | 0.00 | 500.00 |
| 19-21 | 1.79 | 0.00 | 0.00 | 60.00 |
| 22-27 | 5.21 | 0.00 | 0.00 | 240.00 |
| Over 28 | 3.63 | 0.00 | 0.00 | 120.00 |

**Table 2.6.6 In the past week about how much time, in minutes, have you spent using the artificial intelligence applications listed below, or similar such applications? All Other AI Generative Applications. Broken out by urban, suburban or rural upbringing**

| Urban, suburban or rural upbringing | Mean | Median | Minimum | Maximum |
|---|---|---|---|---|
| I grew up in a major city with more than 350,000 people | 3.03 | 0.00 | 0.00 | 240.00 |
| I grew up in a small or medium sized city with less than 350,000 people. | 3.00 | 0.00 | 0.00 | 200.00 |
| I grew up in a suburban area | 4.25 | 0.00 | 0.00 | 500.00 |
| I grew up in a rural area. | 2.17 | 0.00 | 0.00 | 180.00 |
| Unknown | 0.00 | 0.00 | 0.00 | 0.00 |

**Table 2.6.7 In the past week about how much time, in minutes, have you spent using the artificial intelligence applications listed below, or similar such applications? All Other AI Generative Applications. Broken out by region of upbringing**

| Region of upbringing | Mean | Median | Minimum | Maximum |
|---|---|---|---|---|
| The South | 2.44 | 0.00 | 0.00 | 240.00 |
| The Northeast | 2.39 | 0.00 | 0.00 | 180.00 |
| The Midwest | 4.39 | 0.00 | 0.00 | 500.00 |
| The West | 3.26 | 0.00 | 0.00 | 200.00 |
| Abroad | 2.20 | 0.00 | 0.00 | 120.00 |
| Unknown | 0.00 | 0.00 | 0.00 | 0.00 |

**Table 2.6.8 In the past week about how much time, in minutes, have you spent using the artificial intelligence applications listed below, or similar such applications? All Other AI Generative Applications. Broken out by year of class standing**

| Year of class standing | Mean | Median | Minimum | Maximum |
|---|---|---|---|---|
| First year student | 3.25 | 0.00 | 0.00 | 500.00 |
| Sophomore | 2.06 | 0.00 | 0.00 | 180.00 |
| Junior | 2.69 | 0.00 | 0.00 | 200.00 |
| Senior | 4.59 | 0.00 | 0.00 | 240.00 |
| Unknown | 0.00 | 0.00 | 0.00 | 0.00 |

**Table 2.6.9 In the past week about how much time, in minutes, have you spent using the artificial intelligence applications listed below, or similar such applications? All Other AI Generative Applications. Broken out by annual family of origin income level**

| Annual family of origin income level | Mean | Median | Minimum | Maximum |
|---|---|---|---|---|
| Less than $50,000 per year | 2.75 | 0.00 | 0.00 | 200.00 |
| $50,000 to $90,000 per year | 3.09 | 0.00 | 0.00 | 180.00 |
| $90,000+ to $150,000 per year | 4.09 | 0.00 | 0.00 | 500.00 |
| $150,000+ to $250,000 per year | 3.46 | 0.00 | 0.00 | 240.00 |
| More than $250,000 per year | 4.06 | 0.00 | 0.00 | 120.00 |
| Unknown | 0.00 | 0.00 | 0.00 | 0.00 |

**Table 2.6.10 In the past week about how much time, in minutes, have you spent using the artificial intelligence applications listed below, or similar such applications? All Other AI Generative Applications. Broken out by relationship with organized religion**

| Relationship with organized religion | Mean | Median | Minimum | Maximum |
|---|---|---|---|---|
| I practice a religion thoroughly and consider my religion to be a very important part of my life. | 4.74 | 0.00 | 0.00 | 180.00 |
| I practice a religion and try to attend regular services and to participate as much as I can. | 1.77 | 0.00 | 0.00 | 80.00 |
| I identify with a religion but can't say I put a lot of effort into practicing it. | 1.41 | 0.00 | 0.00 | 60.00 |
| I don't really believe in or practice an organized religion. | 4.42 | 0.00 | 0.00 | 500.00 |
| Unknown | 0.00 | 0.00 | 0.00 | 0.00 |

**Table 2.6.11 In the past week about how much time, in minutes, have you spent using the artificial intelligence applications listed below, or similar such applications? All Other AI Generative Applications. Broken out by political views**

| Political views | Mean | Median | Minimum | Maximum |
|---|---|---|---|---|
| Very left wing | 2.01 | 0.00 | 0.00 | 90.00 |
| Liberal | 4.68 | 0.00 | 0.00 | 500.00 |
| Middle of the road | 1.75 | 0.00 | 0.00 | 120.00 |
| Conservative | 4.46 | 0.00 | 0.00 | 180.00 |
| Very right wing | 3.75 | 0.00 | 0.00 | 50.00 |
| Unknown | 0.00 | 0.00 | 0.00 | 0.00 |

**Table 2.6.12 In the past week about how much time, in minutes, have you spent using the artificial intelligence applications listed below, or similar such applications? All Other AI Generative Applications. Broken out by college grades**

| College grades | Mean | Median | Minimum | Maximum |
|---|---|---|---|---|
| A or A- average or more | 3.32 | 0.00 | 0.00 | 500.00 |
| B or B+ average | 3.29 | 0.00 | 0.00 | 200.00 |
| C or C+ or lower | 2.26 | 0.00 | 0.00 | 80.00 |
| Unknown | 0.00 | 0.00 | 0.00 | 0.00 |

**Table 2.6.13 In the past week about how much time, in minutes, have you spent using the artificial intelligence applications listed below, or similar such applications? All Other AI Generative Applications. Broken out by academic major**

| Academic major | Mean | Median | Minimum | Maximum |
|---|---|---|---|---|
| Business, Economics or Finance | 2.22 | 0.00 | 0.00 | 120.00 |
| Psychology | 1.38 | 0.00 | 0.00 | 50.00 |
| Education or Library Science | 12.09 | 0.00 | 0.00 | 500.00 |
| Criminology/Law Enforcement | 2.00 | 0.00 | 0.00 | 30.00 |
| Occupational or Physical Therapy, Nursing, Public Health, Nutrition. other Health-Related | 2.69 | 0.00 | 0.00 | 60.00 |
| Communications, Media, Journalism | 0.00 | 0.00 | 0.00 | 0.00 |
| Fine Arts and Architecture | 6.48 | 0.00 | 0.00 | 180.00 |
| Music, Dance, Theater, other Performing Arts | 4.62 | 0.00 | 0.00 | 120.00 |
| English, Foreign Languages, Comp Literature, Creative Writing | 4.83 | 0.00 | 0.00 | 90.00 |
| Biology, Physics, Chemistry, Pre-Med | 0.83 | 0.00 | 0.00 | 80.00 |
| Geology, Oceanography, Environmental Sciences | 0.00 | 0.00 | 0.00 | 0.00 |
| Engineering, Mathematics, Computer Science | 4.36 | 0.00 | 0.00 | 240.00 |
| History, Classics | 0.00 | 0.00 | 0.00 | 0.00 |
| Sociology, Political Science, Anthropology or other Social Science, except Economics and Psychology | 0.03 | 0.00 | 0.00 | 2.00 |
| Other | 1.54 | 0.00 | 0.00 | 20.00 |

**Table 2.6.14 In the past week about how much time, in minutes, have you spent using the artificial intelligence applications listed below, or similar such applications? All Other AI Generative Applications. Broken out by gender of respondent**

| Gender of respondent | Mean | Median | Minimum | Maximum |
|---|---|---|---|---|
| Male | 3.03 | 0.00 | 0.00 | 240.00 |
| Female | 3.20 | 0.00 | 0.00 | 500.00 |
| Transgender | 5.00 | 0.00 | 0.00 | 90.00 |
| Unknown | 0.00 | 0.00 | 0.00 | 0.00 |

**Table 2.6.15 In the past week about how much time, in minutes, have you spent using the artificial intelligence applications listed below, or similar such applications? All Other AI Generative Applications. Broken out by status of current residency**

| Status of current residency | Mean | Median | Minimum | Maximum |
|---|---|---|---|---|
| At home with my parents or guardian | 2.24 | 0.00 | 0.00 | 200.00 |
| Off campus with others who are not my parents or guardian | 2.86 | 0.00 | 0.00 | 180.00 |
| Off campus alone | 6.26 | 0.00 | 0.00 | 240.00 |
| On campus in the dorms or college-provided suites | 3.18 | 0.00 | 0.00 | 500.00 |
| Unknown | 0.00 | 0.00 | 0.00 | 0.00 |

**Table 2.6.16 In the past week about how much time, in minutes, have you spent using the artificial intelligence applications listed below, or similar such applications? All Other AI Generative Applications. Broken out by current employment situation**

| Current employment situation | Mean | Median | Minimum | Maximum |
|---|---|---|---|---|
| I don't have a full or part time job. | 3.89 | 0.00 | 0.00 | 500.00 |
| I have a part time job. | 2.43 | 0.00 | 0.00 | 200.00 |
| I have a full time job. | 3.95 | 0.00 | 0.00 | 120.00 |
| Unknown | 0.00 | 0.00 | 0.00 | 0.00 |

**Table 2.6.17 In the past week about how much time, in minutes, have you spent using the artificial intelligence applications listed below, or similar such applications? All Other AI Generative Applications. Broken out by sexual orientation**

| Sexual orientation | Mean | Median | Minimum | Maximum |
|---|---|---|---|---|
| Heterosexual or "straight" | 2.76 | 0.00 | 0.00 | 240.00 |
| Homosexual or "gay" | 6.08 | 0.00 | 0.00 | 200.00 |
| Bi-sexual | 3.97 | 0.00 | 0.00 | 500.00 |
| Unknown | 1.33 | 0.00 | 0.00 | 20.00 |

**Table 2.6.18 In the past week about how much time, in minutes, have you spent using the artificial intelligence applications listed below, or similar such applications? All Other AI Generative Applications. Broken out by SAT or ACT score**

| SAT or ACT score | Mean | Median | Minimum | Maximum |
|---|---|---|---|---|
| 30 or over ACT or 1350 or over SAT | 3.71 | 0.00 | 0.00 | 500.00 |
| 24-29 ACT or 1170 to 1349 SAT | 3.31 | 0.00 | 0.00 | 180.00 |
| 20-23 ACT or 1050 to 1169 SAT | 4.39 | 0.00 | 0.00 | 240.00 |
| 17-19 ACT or 900 to 1050 SAT | 2.05 | 0.00 | 0.00 | 120.00 |
| 16 or Under ACT or Under 900 SAT | 0.19 | 0.00 | 0.00 | 5.00 |
| Never took either test | 2.55 | 0.00 | 0.00 | 200.00 |
| Unknown | 1.82 | 0.00 | 0.00 | 20.00 |

**Table 2.6.19 In the past week about how much time, in minutes, have you spent using the artificial intelligence applications listed below, or similar such applications? All Other AI Generative Applications. Broken out by race or ethnicity**

| Race or ethnicity | Mean | Median | Minimum | Maximum |
|---|---|---|---|---|
| White or Caucasian | 2.82 | 0.00 | 0.00 | 180.00 |
| Black or African American | 6.80 | 0.00 | 0.00 | 500.00 |
| Latino or Hispanic | 2.26 | 0.00 | 0.00 | 200.00 |
| Asian or Asian American | 3.15 | 0.00 | 0.00 | 240.00 |
| American Indigenous, Eskimo, Pacific Islander, Hawaiian Native | 0.00 | 0.00 | 0.00 | 0.00 |
| Mixed race | 1.97 | 0.00 | 0.00 | 90.00 |
| Unknown | 0.25 | 0.00 | 0.00 | 3.00 |

**Table 2.6.20 In the past week about how much time, in minutes, have you spent using the artificial intelligence applications listed below, or similar such applications? All Other AI Generative Applications. Broken out by religion**

| Religion | Mean | Median | Minimum | Maximum |
|---|---|---|---|---|
| I do not practice or identify with an organized religion | 2.41 | 0.00 | 0.00 | 200.00 |
| Hinduism | 2.40 | 0.00 | 0.00 | 60.00 |
| Islam | 2.71 | 0.00 | 0.00 | 120.00 |
| Judaism | 0.19 | 0.00 | 0.00 | 5.00 |
| Mormon | 5.00 | 0.00 | 0.00 | 30.00 |
| Catholic | 1.56 | 0.00 | 0.00 | 120.00 |
| Lutheran | 5.16 | 0.00 | 0.00 | 120.00 |
| Baptist | 1.14 | 0.00 | 0.00 | 30.00 |
| Evangelical Protestant Christianity | 8.48 | 0.00 | 0.00 | 120.00 |
| Protestant Christianity | 4.30 | 0.00 | 0.00 | 80.00 |
| Orthodox Christianity | 10.17 | 0.00 | 0.00 | 180.00 |
| Buddhism | 7.00 | 0.00 | 0.00 | 90.00 |
| Non-Denominational Christianity | 7.66 | 0.00 | 0.00 | 500.00 |
| Other | 1.21 | 0.00 | 0.00 | 30.00 |

## Table 3.1 About how important is it to you to learn to use generative artificial intelligence applications effectively?

| | No Answer | Not at all important | Not too important | Somewhat important | Important | Very important |
|---|---|---|---|---|---|---|
| Entire sample | 8.41% | 15.07% | 19.28% | 29.65% | 17.51% | 10.08% |

## Table 3.2 About how important is it to you to learn to use generative artificial intelligence applications effectively? Broken out by tuition of college attended

| Tuition of college attended | No Answer | Not at all important | Not too important | Somewhat important | Important | Very important |
|---|---|---|---|---|---|---|
| Less than $6,000 | 10.11% | 19.10% | 21.35% | 26.97% | 16.10% | 6.37% |
| $6,000+ - $12,000 | 6.91% | 17.48% | 19.51% | 30.89% | 15.04% | 10.16% |
| $12,000+ - $20,000 | 7.63% | 14.89% | 20.61% | 31.68% | 15.27% | 9.92% |
| More than $20,000 | 8.91% | 8.50% | 15.38% | 29.15% | 23.89% | 14.17% |

## Table 3.3 About how important is it to you to learn to use generative artificial intelligence applications effectively? Broken out by enrollment of college attended

| Enrollment of college attended | No Answer | Not at all important | Not too important | Somewhat important | Important | Very important |
|---|---|---|---|---|---|---|
| Less than 5,000 | 8.73% | 10.71% | 15.87% | 29.37% | 21.83% | 13.49% |
| 5,000+ - 12,000 | 6.54% | 14.23% | 17.31% | 35.00% | 17.69% | 9.23% |
| 12,000+ - 22,900 | 8.55% | 16.67% | 23.08% | 27.78% | 14.10% | 9.83% |
| More than 22,900 | 9.78% | 18.48% | 21.01% | 26.45% | 16.30% | 7.97% |

## Table 3.4 About how important is it to you to learn to use generative artificial intelligence applications effectively? Broken out by public or private college

| Public or private college | No Answer | Not at all important | Not too important | Somewhat important | Important | Very important |
|---|---|---|---|---|---|---|
| Public | 8.25% | 16.62% | 20.56% | 29.82% | 15.86% | 8.88% |
| Private | 8.97% | 9.83% | 14.96% | 29.06% | 23.08% | 14.10% |

## Table 3.5 About how important is it to you to learn to use generative artificial intelligence applications effectively? Broken out by age of respondent

| Age of respondent | No Answer | Not at all important | Not too important | Somewhat important | Important | Very important |
|---|---|---|---|---|---|---|
| Under 19 | 10.55% | 14.51% | 20.58% | 30.61% | 17.41% | 6.33% |
| 19-21 | 8.40% | 15.97% | 15.97% | 30.25% | 18.91% | 10.50% |
| 22-27 | 6.64% | 15.17% | 22.27% | 27.49% | 17.06% | 11.37% |
| Over 28 | 6.19% | 14.95% | 17.53% | 29.38% | 16.49% | 15.46% |

## Table 3.6 About how important is it to you to learn to use generative artificial intelligence applications effectively? Broken out by urban, suburban or rural upbringing

| Urban, suburban or rural upbringing | No Answer | Not at all important | Not too important | Somewhat important | Important | Very important |
|---|---|---|---|---|---|---|
| I grew up in a major city with more than 350,000 people | 10.23% | 12.88% | 14.02% | 27.65% | 21.21% | 14.02% |
| I grew up in a small or medium sized city with less than 350,000 people. | 6.30% | 14.57% | 23.62% | 29.53% | 16.14% | 9.84% |
| I grew up in a suburban area | 7.86% | 16.98% | 20.13% | 27.99% | 18.24% | 8.81% |
| I grew up in a rural area. | 8.33% | 15.56% | 19.44% | 36.11% | 13.33% | 7.22% |
| Unknown | 50.00% | 16.67% | 16.67% | 16.67% | 0.00% | 0.00% |

## Table 3.7 About how important is it to you to learn to use generative artificial intelligence applications effectively? Broken out by region of upbringing

| Region of upbringing | No Answer | Not at all important | Not too important | Somewhat important | Important | Very important |
|---|---|---|---|---|---|---|
| The South | 7.76% | 17.96% | 20.00% | 36.73% | 10.61% | 6.94% |
| The Northeast | 8.89% | 16.67% | 25.56% | 21.11% | 18.89% | 8.89% |
| The Midwest | 8.04% | 18.59% | 21.11% | 28.64% | 15.58% | 8.04% |
| The West | 5.93% | 13.56% | 15.25% | 30.51% | 24.58% | 10.17% |
| Abroad | 10.37% | 2.44% | 14.02% | 25.61% | 26.83% | 20.73% |
| Unknown | 42.86% | 14.29% | 0.00% | 28.57% | 14.29% | 0.00% |

## Table 3.8 About how important is it to you to learn to use generative artificial intelligence applications effectively? Broken out by year of class standing

| Year of class standing | No Answer | Not at all important | Not too important | Somewhat important | Important | Very important |
|---|---|---|---|---|---|---|
| First year student | 10.08% | 13.35% | 19.65% | 27.20% | 20.40% | 9.32% |
| Sophomore | 8.89% | 13.33% | 20.00% | 38.89% | 11.11% | 7.78% |
| Junior | 8.77% | 16.96% | 18.71% | 31.58% | 15.79% | 8.19% |
| Senior | 5.04% | 16.67% | 19.77% | 26.36% | 18.99% | 13.18% |
| Unknown | 12.50% | 31.25% | 0.00% | 18.75% | 12.50% | 25.00% |

## Table 3.9 About how important is it to you to learn to use generative artificial intelligence applications effectively? Broken out by annual family of origin income level

| Annual family of origin income level | No Answer | Not at all important | Not too important | Somewhat important | Important | Very important |
|---|---|---|---|---|---|---|
| Less than $50,000 per year | 7.64% | 12.42% | 18.15% | 29.62% | 21.34% | 10.83% |
| $50,000 to $90,000 per year | 7.82% | 19.05% | 19.05% | 29.59% | 14.63% | 9.86% |
| $90,000+ to $150,000 per year | 7.58% | 14.14% | 22.73% | 32.32% | 16.16% | 7.07% |
| $150,000+ to $250,000 per year | 4.81% | 15.38% | 21.15% | 27.88% | 17.31% | 13.46% |
| More than $250,000 per year | 14.44% | 14.44% | 15.56% | 25.56% | 18.89% | 11.11% |
| Unknown | 27.27% | 9.09% | 13.64% | 31.82% | 9.09% | 9.09% |

## Table 3.10 About how important is it to you to learn to use generative artificial intelligence applications effectively? Broken out by relationship with organized religion

| Relationship with organized religion | No Answer | Not at all important | Not too important | Somewhat important | Important | Very important |
|---|---|---|---|---|---|---|
| I practice a religion thoroughly and consider my religion to be a very important part of my life. | 10.71% | 10.20% | 19.39% | 29.08% | 19.39% | 11.22% |
| I practice a religion and try to attend regular services and to participate as much as I can. | 7.01% | 8.92% | 19.75% | 30.57% | 21.66% | 12.10% |
| I identify with a religion but can't say I put a lot of effort into practicing it. | 8.39% | 12.41% | 20.44% | 28.47% | 20.44% | 9.85% |
| I don't really believe in or practice an organized religion. | 6.98% | 22.22% | 18.09% | 30.49% | 13.18% | 9.04% |
| Unknown | 50.00% | 0.00% | 25.00% | 25.00% | 0.00% | 0.00% |

## Table 3.11 About how important is it to you to learn to use generative artificial intelligence applications effectively? Broken out by political views

| Political views | No Answer | Not at all important | Not too important | Somewhat important | Important | Very important |
|---|---|---|---|---|---|---|
| Very left wing | 9.93% | 25.17% | 15.89% | 29.14% | 12.58% | 7.28% |
| Liberal | 7.05% | 15.72% | 19.24% | 28.18% | 18.97% | 10.84% |
| Middle of the road | 7.76% | 11.34% | 19.40% | 31.64% | 18.51% | 11.34% |
| Conservative | 10.87% | 11.59% | 23.19% | 31.16% | 15.22% | 7.97% |
| Very right wing | 5.00% | 15.00% | 20.00% | 25.00% | 20.00% | 15.00% |
| Unknown | 33.33% | 11.11% | 11.11% | 11.11% | 33.33% | 0.00% |

## Table 3.12 About how important is it to you to learn to use generative artificial intelligence applications effectively? Broken out by college grades

| College grades | No Answer | Not at all important | Not too important | Somewhat important | Important | Very important |
|---|---|---|---|---|---|---|
| A or A- average or more | 7.33% | 14.20% | 18.32% | 29.92% | 19.54% | 10.69% |
| B or B+ average | 8.64% | 16.61% | 21.93% | 29.90% | 14.62% | 8.31% |
| C or C+ or lower | 12.90% | 17.74% | 17.74% | 27.42% | 11.29% | 12.90% |
| Unknown | 100.00% | 0.00% | 0.00% | 0.00% | 0.00% | 0.00% |

## Table 3.13 About how important is it to you to learn to use generative artificial intelligence applications effectively? Broken out by academic major

| Academic major | No Answer | Not at all important | Not too important | Somewhat important | Important | Very important |
|---|---|---|---|---|---|---|
| Business, Economics or Finance | 8.73% | 8.73% | 15.87% | 33.33% | 26.19% | 7.14% |
| Psychology | 7.45% | 22.34% | 21.28% | 28.72% | 10.64% | 9.57% |
| Education or Library Science | 6.76% | 17.57% | 22.97% | 29.73% | 14.86% | 8.11% |
| Criminology/Law Enforcement | 0.00% | 40.00% | 13.33% | 6.67% | 33.33% | 6.67% |
| Occupational or Physical Therapy, Nursing, Public Health, Nutrition. other Health-Related | 7.41% | 12.04% | 27.78% | 35.19% | 11.11% | 6.48% |
| Communications, Media, Journalism | 12.50% | 12.50% | 16.67% | 29.17% | 8.33% | 20.83% |
| Fine Arts and Architecture | 9.52% | 20.63% | 33.33% | 20.63% | 14.29% | 1.59% |
| Music, Dance, Theater, other Performing Arts | 3.85% | 30.77% | 15.38% | 26.92% | 23.08% | 0.00% |
| English, Foreign Languages, Comp Literature, Creative Writing | 10.34% | 27.59% | 17.24% | 27.59% | 10.34% | 6.90% |
| Biology, Physics, Chemistry, Pre-Med | 10.53% | 17.29% | 16.54% | 30.83% | 15.04% | 9.77% |
| Geology, Oceanography, Environmental Sciences | 11.54% | 19.23% | 34.62% | 23.08% | 7.69% | 3.85% |
| Engineering, Mathematics, Computer Science | 7.43% | 6.93% | 15.84% | 26.24% | 26.24% | 17.33% |
| History, Classics | 7.69% | 23.08% | 7.69% | 38.46% | 7.69% | 15.38% |
| Sociology, Political Science, Anthropology or other Social Science, except Economics and Psychology | 9.21% | 13.16% | 11.84% | 38.16% | 13.16% | 14.47% |
| Other | 15.38% | 23.08% | 7.69% | 30.77% | 15.38% | 7.69% |

## Table 3.14 About how important is it to you to learn to use generative artificial intelligence applications effectively? Broken out by gender of respondent

| Gender of respondent | No Answer | Not at all important | Not too important | Somewhat important | Important | Very important |
|---|---|---|---|---|---|---|
| Male | 7.89% | 10.82% | 18.13% | 28.65% | 21.35% | 13.16% |
| Female | 8.55% | 15.32% | 19.19% | 32.26% | 16.13% | 8.55% |
| Transgender | 7.02% | 38.60% | 26.32% | 8.77% | 10.53% | 8.77% |
| Unknown | 66.67% | 0.00% | 33.33% | 0.00% | 0.00% | 0.00% |

## Table 3.15 About how important is it to you to learn to use generative artificial intelligence applications effectively? Broken out by status of current residency

| Status of current residency | No Answer | Not at all important | Not too important | Somewhat important | Important | Very important |
|---|---|---|---|---|---|---|
| At home with my parents or guardian | 9.05% | 17.19% | 23.98% | 28.96% | 12.67% | 8.14% |
| Off campus with others who are not my parents or guardian | 6.35% | 14.29% | 20.24% | 32.14% | 16.67% | 10.32% |
| Off campus alone | 6.96% | 13.91% | 18.26% | 22.61% | 22.61% | 15.65% |
| On campus in the dorms or college-provided suites | 9.28% | 14.85% | 16.47% | 30.63% | 19.26% | 9.51% |
| Unknown | 66.67% | 0.00% | 33.33% | 0.00% | 0.00% | 0.00% |

## Table 3.16 About how important is it to you to learn to use generative artificial intelligence applications effectively? Broken out by current employment situation

| Current employment situation | No Answer | Not at all important | Not too important | Somewhat important | Important | Very important |
|---|---|---|---|---|---|---|
| I don't have a full or part time job. | 9.42% | 13.29% | 19.81% | 28.99% | 19.57% | 8.94% |
| I have a part time job. | 7.78% | 15.56% | 18.44% | 31.11% | 15.56% | 11.56% |
| I have a full time job. | 5.92% | 19.08% | 21.05% | 26.97% | 17.76% | 9.21% |
| Unknown | 50.00% | 0.00% | 0.00% | 33.33% | 16.67% | 0.00% |

## Table 3.17 About how important is it to you to learn to use generative artificial intelligence applications effectively? Broken out by sexual orientation

| Sexual orientation | No Answer | Not at all important | Not too important | Somewhat important | Important | Very important |
|---|---|---|---|---|---|---|
| Heterosexual or "straight" | 8.34% | 11.27% | 20.17% | 29.07% | 19.61% | 11.54% |
| Homosexual or "gay" | 5.41% | 27.03% | 16.22% | 28.38% | 14.86% | 8.11% |
| Bi-sexual | 7.94% | 24.30% | 18.22% | 32.71% | 10.75% | 6.07% |
| Unknown | 33.33% | 6.67% | 6.67% | 20.00% | 26.67% | 6.67% |

## Table 3.18 About how important is it to you to learn to use generative artificial intelligence applications effectively? Broken out by SAT or ACT score

| SAT or ACT score | No Answer | Not at all important | Not too important | Somewhat important | Important | Very important |
|---|---|---|---|---|---|---|
| 30 or over ACT or 1350 or over SAT | 5.98% | 16.73% | 15.54% | 29.08% | 19.12% | 13.55% |
| 24-29 ACT or 1170 to 1349 SAT | 8.17% | 19.07% | 19.84% | 30.35% | 15.56% | 7.00% |
| 20-23 ACT or 1050 to 1169 SAT | 7.78% | 16.11% | 27.22% | 28.89% | 15.00% | 5.00% |
| 17-19 ACT or 900 to 1050 SAT | 12.50% | 14.77% | 15.91% | 34.09% | 17.05% | 5.68% |
| 16 or Under ACT or Under 900 SAT | 11.11% | 3.70% | 14.81% | 40.74% | 18.52% | 11.11% |
| Never took either test | 9.13% | 9.62% | 18.27% | 26.44% | 20.19% | 16.35% |
| Unknown | 27.27% | 0.00% | 18.18% | 36.36% | 18.18% | 0.00% |

## Table 3.19 About how important is it to you to learn to use generative artificial intelligence applications effectively? Broken out by race or ethnicity

| Race or ethnicity | No Answer | Not at all important | Not too important | Somewhat important | Important | Very important |
|---|---|---|---|---|---|---|
| White or Caucasian | 7.13% | 19.65% | 23.70% | 27.55% | 13.68% | 8.29% |
| Black or African American | 12.03% | 11.28% | 14.29% | 30.08% | 20.30% | 12.03% |
| Latino or Hispanic | 8.65% | 14.42% | 21.15% | 33.65% | 16.35% | 5.77% |
| Asian or Asian American | 8.99% | 5.06% | 14.04% | 31.46% | 25.28% | 15.17% |
| American Indigenous, Eskimo, Pacific Islander, Hawaiian Native | 0.00% | 40.00% | 0.00% | 20.00% | 20.00% | 20.00% |
| Mixed race | 8.45% | 15.49% | 7.04% | 32.39% | 22.54% | 14.08% |
| Unknown | 16.67% | 0.00% | 25.00% | 41.67% | 16.67% | 0.00% |

## Table 3.20 About how important is it to you to learn to use generative artificial intelligence applications effectively? Broken out by religion

| Religion | No Answer | Not at all important | Not too important | Somewhat important | Important | Very important |
|---|---|---|---|---|---|---|
| I do not practice or identify with an organized religion | 7.09% | 19.95% | 18.37% | 30.18% | 14.44% | 9.97% |
| Hinduism | 10.00% | 6.00% | 18.00% | 28.00% | 22.00% | 16.00% |
| Islam | 12.50% | 12.50% | 8.33% | 27.08% | 27.08% | 12.50% |
| Judaism | 11.11% | 11.11% | 7.41% | 40.74% | 22.22% | 7.41% |
| Mormon | 0.00% | 16.67% | 0.00% | 33.33% | 50.00% | 0.00% |
| Catholic | 8.15% | 12.59% | 22.22% | 28.89% | 19.26% | 8.89% |
| Lutheran | 21.88% | 3.13% | 31.25% | 25.00% | 12.50% | 6.25% |
| Baptist | 11.11% | 20.63% | 15.87% | 33.33% | 15.87% | 3.17% |
| Evangelical Protestant Christianity | 0.00% | 4.35% | 30.43% | 34.78% | 13.04% | 17.39% |
| Protestant Christianity | 4.00% | 14.00% | 28.00% | 20.00% | 20.00% | 14.00% |
| Orthodox Christianity | 5.56% | 11.11% | 16.67% | 27.78% | 27.78% | 11.11% |
| Buddhism | 0.00% | 5.00% | 10.00% | 40.00% | 25.00% | 20.00% |
| Non-Denominational Christianity | 9.01% | 15.32% | 25.23% | 30.63% | 13.51% | 6.31% |
| Other | 12.07% | 10.34% | 13.79% | 25.86% | 22.41% | 15.52% |

## Table 4.1 Do you have a paid subscription to ChatGPT?

| | No Answer | Yes | No |
|---|---|---|---|
| Entire sample | 8.22% | 8.12% | 83.66% |

## Table 4.2 Do you have a paid subscription to ChatGPT? Broken out by tuition of college attended

| Tuition of college attended | No Answer | Yes | No |
|---|---|---|---|
| Less than $6,000 | 9.74% | 5.62% | 84.64% |
| $6,000+ - $12,000 | 6.10% | 4.07% | 89.84% |
| $12,000+ - $20,000 | 8.02% | 9.54% | 82.44% |
| More than $20,000 | 8.91% | 13.36% | 77.73% |

## Table 4.3 Do you have a paid subscription to ChatGPT? Broken out by enrollment of college attended

| Enrollment of college attended | No Answer | Yes | No |
|---|---|---|---|
| Less than 5,000 | 8.73% | 11.90% | 79.37% |
| 5,000+ - 12,000 | 6.92% | 6.15% | 86.92% |
| 12,000+ - 22,900 | 7.69% | 8.97% | 83.33% |
| More than 22,900 | 9.42% | 5.80% | 84.78% |

## Table 4.4 Do you have a paid subscription to ChatGPT? Broken out by public or private college

| Public or private college | No Answer | Yes | No |
|---|---|---|---|
| Public | 7.99% | 6.60% | 85.41% |
| Private | 8.97% | 13.25% | 77.78% |

## Table 4.5 Do you have a paid subscription to ChatGPT? Broken out by age of respondent

| Age of respondent | No Answer | Yes | No |
|---|---|---|---|
| Under 19 | 10.03% | 3.96% | 86.02% |
| 19-21 | 8.40% | 6.72% | 84.87% |
| 22-27 | 7.11% | 11.37% | 81.52% |
| Over 28 | 5.67% | 14.43% | 79.90% |

## Table 4.6 Do you have a paid subscription to ChatGPT? Broken out by urban, suburban or rural upbringing

| Urban, suburban or rural upbringing | No Answer | Yes | No |
|---|---|---|---|
| I grew up in a major city with more than 350,000 people | 10.23% | 10.61% | 79.17% |
| I grew up in a small or medium sized city with less than 350,000 people. | 6.30% | 8.66% | 85.04% |
| I grew up in a suburban area | 7.86% | 7.23% | 84.91% |
| I grew up in a rural area. | 7.22% | 5.56% | 87.22% |
| Unknown | 50.00% | 0.00% | 50.00% |

## Table 4.7 Do you have a paid subscription to ChatGPT? Broken out by region of upbringing

| Region of upbringing | No Answer | Yes | No |
|---|---|---|---|
| The South | 7.76% | 4.90% | 87.35% |
| The Northeast | 8.89% | 6.67% | 84.44% |
| The Midwest | 7.79% | 5.28% | 86.93% |
| The West | 5.93% | 8.47% | 85.59% |
| Abroad | 10.37% | 20.12% | 69.51% |
| Unknown | 28.57% | 14.29% | 57.14% |

## Table 4.8 Do you have a paid subscription to ChatGPT? Broken out by year of class standing

| Year of class standing | No Answer | Yes | No |
|---|---|---|---|
| First year student | 9.57% | 5.04% | 85.39% |
| Sophomore | 8.33% | 6.11% | 85.56% |
| Junior | 8.77% | 7.60% | 83.63% |
| Senior | 5.43% | 14.73% | 79.84% |
| Unknown | 12.50% | 6.25% | 81.25% |

## Table 4.9 Do you have a paid subscription to ChatGPT? Broken out by annual family of origin income level

| Annual family of origin income level | No Answer | Yes | No |
|---|---|---|---|
| Less than $50,000 per year | 7.64% | 11.15% | 81.21% |
| $50,000 to $90,000 per year | 7.82% | 4.42% | 87.76% |
| $90,000+ to $150,000 per year | 7.58% | 5.05% | 87.37% |
| $150,000+ to $250,000 per year | 3.85% | 16.35% | 79.81% |
| More than $250,000 per year | 14.44% | 8.89% | 76.67% |
| Unknown | 22.73% | 0.00% | 77.27% |

## Table 4.10 Do you have a paid subscription to ChatGPT? Broken out by relationship with organized religion

| Relationship with organized religion | No Answer | Yes | No |
|---|---|---|---|
| I practice a religion thoroughly and consider my religion to be a very important part of my life. | 10.71% | 7.14% | 82.14% |
| I practice a religion and try to attend regular services and to participate as much as I can. | 6.37% | 7.64% | 85.99% |
| I identify with a religion but can't say I put a lot of effort into practicing it. | 8.39% | 8.03% | 83.58% |
| I don't really believe in or practice an organized religion. | 6.98% | 9.04% | 83.98% |
| Unknown | 37.50% | 0.00% | 62.50% |

## Table 4.11 Do you have a paid subscription to ChatGPT? Broken out by political views

| Political views | No Answer | Yes | No |
|---|---|---|---|
| Very left wing | 9.27% | 7.28% | 83.44% |
| Liberal | 7.05% | 7.32% | 85.64% |
| Middle of the road | 7.76% | 9.85% | 82.39% |
| Conservative | 10.87% | 5.80% | 83.33% |
| Very right wing | 5.00% | 15.00% | 80.00% |
| Unknown | 22.22% | 11.11% | 66.67% |

## Table 4.12 Do you have a paid subscription to ChatGPT? Broken out by college grades

| College grades | No Answer | Yes | No |
|---|---|---|---|
| A or A- average or more | 7.48% | 9.77% | 82.75% |
| B or B+ average | 7.97% | 6.31% | 85.71% |
| C or C+ or lower | 11.29% | 0.00% | 88.71% |
| Unknown | 100.00% | 0.00% | 0.00% |

## Table 4.13 Do you have a paid subscription to ChatGPT? Broken out by academic major

| Academic major | No Answer | Yes | No |
|---|---|---|---|
| Business, Economics or Finance | 8.73% | 11.11% | 80.16% |
| Psychology | 7.45% | 5.32% | 87.23% |
| Education or Library Science | 6.76% | 2.70% | 90.54% |
| Criminology/Law Enforcement | 0.00% | 0.00% | 100.00% |
| Occupational or Physical Therapy, Nursing, Public Health, Nutrition. other Health-Related | 6.48% | 10.19% | 83.33% |
| Communications, Media, Journalism | 12.50% | 4.17% | 83.33% |
| Fine Arts and Architecture | 9.52% | 1.59% | 88.89% |
| Music, Dance, Theater, other Performing Arts | 3.85% | 3.85% | 92.31% |
| English, Foreign Languages, Comp Literature, Creative Writing | 6.90% | 10.34% | 82.76% |
| Biology, Physics, Chemistry, Pre-Med | 12.03% | 5.26% | 82.71% |
| Geology, Oceanography, Environmental Sciences | 11.54% | 7.69% | 80.77% |
| Engineering, Mathematics, Computer Science | 7.43% | 14.85% | 77.72% |
| History, Classics | 7.69% | 0.00% | 92.31% |
| Sociology, Political Science, Anthropology or other Social Science, except Economics and Psychology | 6.58% | 7.89% | 85.53% |
| Other | 15.38% | 0.00% | 84.62% |

## Table 4.14 Do you have a paid subscription to ChatGPT? Broken out by gender of respondent

| Gender of respondent | No Answer | Yes | No |
|---|---|---|---|
| Male | 8.19% | 13.16% | 78.65% |
| Female | 8.06% | 5.65% | 86.29% |
| Transgender | 7.02% | 5.26% | 87.72% |
| Unknown | 66.67% | 0.00% | 33.33% |

## Table 4.15 Do you have a paid subscription to ChatGPT? Broken out by status of current residency

| Status of current residency | No Answer | Yes | No |
|---|---|---|---|
| At home with my parents or guardian | 9.50% | 5.43% | 85.07% |
| Off campus with others who are not my parents or guardian | 6.35% | 10.32% | 83.33% |
| Off campus alone | 6.96% | 15.65% | 77.39% |
| On campus in the dorms or college-provided suites | 8.58% | 6.26% | 85.15% |
| Unknown | 66.67% | 0.00% | 33.33% |

## Table 4.16 Do you have a paid subscription to ChatGPT? Broken out by current employment situation

| Current employment situation | No Answer | Yes | No |
|---|---|---|---|
| I don't have a full or part time job. | 9.18% | 9.18% | 81.64% |
| I have a part time job. | 7.56% | 7.33% | 85.11% |
| I have a full time job. | 5.92% | 7.89% | 86.18% |
| Unknown | 50.00% | 0.00% | 50.00% |

## Table 4.17 Do you have a paid subscription to ChatGPT? Broken out by sexual orientation

| Sexual orientation | No Answer | Yes | No |
|---|---|---|---|
| Heterosexual or "straight" | 8.21% | 8.62% | 83.17% |
| Homosexual or "gay" | 5.41% | 12.16% | 82.43% |
| Bi-sexual | 7.48% | 5.61% | 86.92% |
| Unknown | 33.33% | 0.00% | 66.67% |

## Table 4.18 Do you have a paid subscription to ChatGPT? Broken out by SAT or ACT score

| SAT or ACT score | No Answer | Yes | No |
|---|---|---|---|
| 30 or over ACT or 1350 or over SAT | 5.98% | 11.55% | 82.47% |
| 24-29 ACT or 1170 to 1349 SAT | 8.56% | 5.84% | 85.60% |
| 20-23 ACT or 1050 to 1169 SAT | 8.33% | 7.22% | 84.44% |
| 17-19 ACT or 900 to 1050 SAT | 10.23% | 2.27% | 87.50% |
| 16 or Under ACT or Under 900 SAT | 7.41% | 0.00% | 92.59% |
| Never took either test | 8.65% | 11.54% | 79.81% |
| Unknown | 27.27% | 0.00% | 72.73% |

## Table 4.19 Do you have a paid subscription to ChatGPT? Broken out by race or ethnicity

| Race or ethnicity | No Answer | Yes | No |
|---|---|---|---|
| White or Caucasian | 6.94% | 7.13% | 85.93% |
| Black or African American | 11.28% | 4.51% | 84.21% |
| Latino or Hispanic | 8.65% | 7.69% | 83.65% |
| Asian or Asian American | 9.55% | 14.61% | 75.84% |
| American Indigenous, Eskimo, Pacific Islander, Hawaiian Native | 0.00% | 0.00% | 100.00% |
| Mixed race | 7.04% | 8.45% | 84.51% |
| Unknown | 16.67% | 0.00% | 83.33% |

## Table 4.20 Do you have a paid subscription to ChatGPT? Broken out by religion

| Religion | No Answer | Yes | No |
|---|---|---|---|
| I do not practice or identify with an organized religion | 6.82% | 7.35% | 85.83% |
| Hinduism | 10.00% | 12.00% | 78.00% |
| Islam | 12.50% | 16.67% | 70.83% |
| Judaism | 11.11% | 18.52% | 70.37% |
| Mormon | 0.00% | 16.67% | 83.33% |
| Catholic | 6.67% | 3.70% | 89.63% |
| Lutheran | 21.88% | 9.38% | 68.75% |
| Baptist | 11.11% | 6.35% | 82.54% |
| Evangelical Protestant Christianity | 0.00% | 13.04% | 86.96% |
| Protestant Christianity | 4.00% | 8.00% | 88.00% |
| Orthodox Christianity | 5.56% | 11.11% | 83.33% |
| Buddhism | 0.00% | 20.00% | 80.00% |
| Non-Denominational Christianity | 9.91% | 6.31% | 83.78% |
| Other | 12.07% | 5.17% | 82.76% |

## Table 5.1 Do you have a personal paid subscription to any other generative AI application other than ChatGPT?

| | No Answer | Yes | No |
|---|---|---|---|
| Entire sample | 8.12% | 2.25% | 89.63% |

## Table 5.2 Do you have a personal paid subscription to any other generative AI application other than ChatGPT? Broken out by tuition of college attended

| Tuition of college attended | No Answer | Yes | No |
|---|---|---|---|
| Less than $6,000 | 9.74% | 1.12% | 89.14% |
| $6,000+ - $12,000 | 6.50% | 2.03% | 91.46% |
| $12,000+ - $20,000 | 7.63% | 4.20% | 88.17% |
| More than $20,000 | 8.50% | 1.62% | 89.88% |

## Table 5.3 Do you have a personal paid subscription to any other generative AI application other than ChatGPT? Broken out by enrollment of college attended

| Enrollment of college attended | No Answer | Yes | No |
|---|---|---|---|
| Less than 5,000 | 8.33% | 1.59% | 90.08% |
| 5,000+ - 12,000 | 6.54% | 2.69% | 90.77% |
| 12,000+ - 22,900 | 8.12% | 3.42% | 88.46% |
| More than 22,900 | 9.42% | 1.45% | 89.13% |

## Table 5.4 Do you have a personal paid subscription to any other generative AI application other than ChatGPT? Broken out by public or private college

| Public or private college | No Answer | Yes | No |
|---|---|---|---|
| Public | 7.99% | 2.41% | 89.59% |
| Private | 8.55% | 1.71% | 89.74% |

## Table 5.5 Do you have a personal paid subscription to any other generative AI application other than ChatGPT? Broken out by age of respondent

| Age of respondent | No Answer | Yes | No |
|---|---|---|---|
| Under 19 | 10.03% | 1.06% | 88.92% |
| 19-21 | 8.40% | 1.26% | 90.34% |
| 22-27 | 6.64% | 3.32% | 90.05% |
| Over 28 | 5.67% | 4.64% | 89.69% |

## Table 5.6 Do you have a personal paid subscription to any other generative AI application other than ChatGPT? Broken out by urban, suburban or rural upbringing

| Urban, suburban or rural upbringing | No Answer | Yes | No |
|---|---|---|---|
| I grew up in a major city with more than 350,000 people | 10.23% | 2.65% | 87.12% |
| I grew up in a small or medium sized city with less than 350,000 people. | 5.91% | 3.15% | 90.94% |
| I grew up in a suburban area | 7.55% | 1.89% | 90.57% |
| I grew up in a rural area. | 7.78% | 1.11% | 91.11% |
| Unknown | 50.00% | 0.00% | 50.00% |

## Table 5.7 Do you have a personal paid subscription to any other generative AI application other than ChatGPT? Broken out by region of upbringing

| Region of upbringing | No Answer | Yes | No |
|---|---|---|---|
| The South | 7.35% | 1.63% | 91.02% |
| The Northeast | 8.89% | 3.33% | 87.78% |
| The Midwest | 7.79% | 1.51% | 90.70% |
| The West | 5.93% | 0.85% | 93.22% |
| Abroad | 10.37% | 5.49% | 84.15% |
| Unknown | 28.57% | 0.00% | 71.43% |

## Table 5.8 Do you have a personal paid subscription to any other generative AI application other than ChatGPT? Broken out by year of class standing

| Year of class standing | No Answer | Yes | No |
|---|---|---|---|
| First year student | 9.57% | 1.51% | 88.92% |
| Sophomore | 8.33% | 0.56% | 91.11% |
| Junior | 8.77% | 5.26% | 85.96% |
| Senior | 5.04% | 2.71% | 92.25% |
| Unknown | 12.50% | 0.00% | 87.50% |

## Table 5.9 Do you have a personal paid subscription to any other generative AI application other than ChatGPT? Broken out by annual family of origin income level

| Annual family of origin income level | No Answer | Yes | No |
|---|---|---|---|
| Less than $50,000 per year | 7.64% | 3.18% | 89.17% |
| $50,000 to $90,000 per year | 7.48% | 1.36% | 91.16% |
| $90,000+ to $150,000 per year | 7.58% | 2.02% | 90.40% |
| $150,000+ to $250,000 per year | 3.85% | 1.92% | 94.23% |
| More than $250,000 per year | 14.44% | 3.33% | 82.22% |
| Unknown | 22.73% | 0.00% | 77.27% |

## Table 5.10 Do you have a personal paid subscription to any other generative AI application other than ChatGPT? Broken out by relationship with organized religion

| Relationship with organized religion | No Answer | Yes | No |
|---|---|---|---|
| I practice a religion thoroughly and consider my religion to be a very important part of my life. | 10.71% | 3.06% | 86.22% |
| I practice a religion and try to attend regular services and to participate as much as I can. | 7.01% | 2.55% | 90.45% |
| I identify with a religion but can't say I put a lot of effort into practicing it. | 8.03% | 2.19% | 89.78% |
| I don't really believe in or practice an organized religion. | 6.72% | 1.81% | 91.47% |
| Unknown | 37.50% | 0.00% | 62.50% |

## Table 5.11 Do you have a personal paid subscription to any other generative AI application other than ChatGPT? Broken out by political views

| Political views | No Answer | Yes | No |
|---|---|---|---|
| Very left wing | 9.27% | 2.65% | 88.08% |
| Liberal | 6.78% | 0.81% | 92.41% |
| Middle of the road | 7.76% | 3.58% | 88.66% |
| Conservative | 10.87% | 1.45% | 87.68% |
| Very right wing | 5.00% | 10.00% | 85.00% |
| Unknown | 22.22% | 0.00% | 77.78% |

## Table 5.12 Do you have a personal paid subscription to any other generative AI application other than ChatGPT? Broken out by college grades

| College grades | No Answer | Yes | No |
|---|---|---|---|
| A or A- average or more | 7.33% | 1.98% | 90.69% |
| B or B+ average | 7.97% | 2.99% | 89.04% |
| C or C+ or lower | 11.29% | 1.61% | 87.10% |
| Unknown | 100.00% | 0.00% | 0.00% |

## Table 5.13 Do you have a personal paid subscription to any other generative AI application other than ChatGPT? Broken out by academic major

| Academic major | No Answer | Yes | No |
|---|---|---|---|
| Business, Economics or Finance | 8.73% | 0.79% | 90.48% |
| Psychology | 7.45% | 2.13% | 90.43% |
| Education or Library Science | 6.76% | 1.35% | 91.89% |
| Criminology/Law Enforcement | 0.00% | 0.00% | 100.00% |
| Occupational or Physical Therapy, Nursing, Public Health, Nutrition. other Health-Related | 7.41% | 2.78% | 89.81% |
| Communications, Media, Journalism | 12.50% | 4.17% | 83.33% |
| Fine Arts and Architecture | 9.52% | 3.17% | 87.30% |
| Music, Dance, Theater, other Performing Arts | 3.85% | 3.85% | 92.31% |
| English, Foreign Languages, Comp Literature, Creative Writing | 6.90% | 3.45% | 89.66% |
| Biology, Physics, Chemistry, Pre-Med | 10.53% | 1.50% | 87.97% |
| Geology, Oceanography, Environmental Sciences | 11.54% | 0.00% | 88.46% |
| Engineering, Mathematics, Computer Science | 7.43% | 3.47% | 89.11% |
| History, Classics | 7.69% | 0.00% | 92.31% |
| Sociology, Political Science, Anthropology or other Social Science, except Economics and Psychology | 6.58% | 2.63% | 90.79% |
| Other | 15.38% | 0.00% | 84.62% |

## Table 5.14 Do you have a personal paid subscription to any other generative AI application other than ChatGPT? Broken out by gender of respondent

| Gender of respondent | No Answer | Yes | No |
|---|---|---|---|
| Male | 7.89% | 3.22% | 88.89% |
| Female | 8.06% | 1.77% | 90.16% |
| Transgender | 7.02% | 1.75% | 91.23% |
| Unknown | 66.67% | 0.00% | 33.33% |

## Table 5.15 Do you have a personal paid subscription to any other generative AI application other than ChatGPT? Broken out by status of current residency

| Status of current residency | No Answer | Yes | No |
|---|---|---|---|
| At home with my parents or guardian | 9.05% | 1.81% | 89.14% |
| Off campus with others who are not my parents or guardian | 6.35% | 3.17% | 90.48% |
| Off campus alone | 6.96% | 3.48% | 89.57% |
| On campus in the dorms or college-provided suites | 8.58% | 1.62% | 89.79% |
| Unknown | 66.67% | 0.00% | 33.33% |

## Table 5.16 Do you have a personal paid subscription to any other generative AI application other than ChatGPT? Broken out by current employment situation

| Current employment situation | No Answer | Yes | No |
|---|---|---|---|
| I don't have a full or part time job. | 8.70% | 1.69% | 89.61% |
| I have a part time job. | 7.78% | 2.67% | 89.56% |
| I have a full time job. | 5.92% | 2.63% | 91.45% |
| Unknown | 50.00% | 0.00% | 50.00% |

## Table 5.17 Do you have a personal paid subscription to any other generative AI application other than ChatGPT? Broken out by sexual orientation

| Sexual orientation | No Answer | Yes | No |
|---|---|---|---|
| Heterosexual or "straight" | 8.07% | 2.50% | 89.43% |
| Homosexual or "gay" | 5.41% | 2.70% | 91.89% |
| Bi-sexual | 7.48% | 1.40% | 91.12% |
| Unknown | 33.33% | 0.00% | 66.67% |

## Table 5.18 Do you have a personal paid subscription to any other generative AI application other than ChatGPT? Broken out by SAT or ACT score

| SAT or ACT score | No Answer | Yes | No |
|---|---|---|---|
| 30 or over ACT or 1350 or over SAT | 5.98% | 2.39% | 91.63% |
| 24-29 ACT or 1170 to 1349 SAT | 8.17% | 1.95% | 89.88% |
| 20-23 ACT or 1050 to 1169 SAT | 7.78% | 2.78% | 89.44% |
| 17-19 ACT or 900 to 1050 SAT | 11.36% | 3.41% | 85.23% |
| 16 or Under ACT or Under 900 SAT | 7.41% | 0.00% | 92.59% |
| Never took either test | 8.65% | 1.92% | 89.42% |
| Unknown | 27.27% | 0.00% | 72.73% |

## Table 5.19 Do you have a personal paid subscription to any other generative AI application other than ChatGPT? Broken out by race or ethnicity

| Race or ethnicity | No Answer | Yes | No |
|---|---|---|---|
| White or Caucasian | 7.13% | 1.73% | 91.14% |
| Black or African American | 11.28% | 1.50% | 87.22% |
| Latino or Hispanic | 7.69% | 1.92% | 90.38% |
| Asian or Asian American | 8.99% | 5.06% | 85.96% |
| American Indigenous, Eskimo, Pacific Islander, Hawaiian Native | 0.00% | 0.00% | 100.00% |
| Mixed race | 7.04% | 0.00% | 92.96% |
| Unknown | 16.67% | 8.33% | 75.00% |

## Table 5.20 Do you have a personal paid subscription to any other generative AI application other than ChatGPT? Broken out by religion

| Religion | No Answer | Yes | No |
|---|---|---|---|
| I do not practice or identify with an organized religion | 6.56% | 1.84% | 91.60% |
| Hinduism | 10.00% | 4.00% | 86.00% |
| Islam | 12.50% | 4.17% | 83.33% |
| Judaism | 11.11% | 0.00% | 88.89% |
| Mormon | 0.00% | 0.00% | 100.00% |
| Catholic | 7.41% | 0.00% | 92.59% |
| Lutheran | 21.88% | 6.25% | 71.88% |
| Baptist | 11.11% | 0.00% | 88.89% |
| Evangelical Protestant Christianity | 0.00% | 13.04% | 86.96% |
| Protestant Christianity | 4.00% | 2.00% | 94.00% |
| Orthodox Christianity | 5.56% | 11.11% | 83.33% |
| Buddhism | 0.00% | 5.00% | 95.00% |
| Non-Denominational Christianity | 9.01% | 0.90% | 90.09% |
| Other | 12.07% | 3.45% | 84.48% |

## What do you primarily use artificial intelligence applications for?

Business, Economics or Finance

1 To boost my writing and grammar.
2 I used to use ChatGPT sometimes to have it argue against me to refine my arguments for debate, but I found its responses to be largely generic and unhelpful, so I haven't used it in months. I think the last time I used it was to ask why some random policy could be considered unconstitutional.
3 School research
4 I use it for generating ideas for crafts
5 Looking up answers for hard questions or giving me ideas.
6 I use Copilot to generate ideas and creative material usually since it provides free access to GPT4. I use Gemini as part of Google's search engine to receive summaries on info I want to learn more about. I use Suno and Luma to generate and experiment with creative content like music and videos respectively.
7 It's useful for creating frameworks for projects and papers as well as a creativity tool. However, the writing it produces is substandard and markedly AI written. AI is also useful recreationally for arguing a large range of issues cogently.
8 A lot of general questions I have or answered by AI. Also during school, AI usually does a good job of explaining topics and concepts that I have a hard time understanding.
9 Confirming basic information or rewording phrases
10 Supplemental studying material and feedback for personal creative writing
11 Assistance with writing and schoolwork
12 Homework and writing help
13 Proofreading
14 To help me better understand concepts that I struggle with that my class or class materials (textbooks or slides) does not cover the best or if I need a different way of understanding it.
15 Ideas
16 Research, information
17 Clarification on assignments
18 I do not use artificial intelligence.
19 Writing help with ideas and concision, random questions that I have.
20 Research and study
21 In my work life, I use it to help me generate captions for social media posts. In my school life, I use it for idea generation and to help me gather my thoughts.
22 I don't.
23 For assignment
24 ChatGPT
25 I don't

26 Nothing, if I can help it. I believe that generative AI is theft, and I've experienced that theft firsthand, being an artist who posts my art online.
27 Cooking recipes and alternatives in recipes, questions I had most recently I couldn't find on the internet In regard to career decisions and AI gave me a useful answer.
28 School
29 School
30 Help generate ideas.
31 Assignments and letters
32 I don't really use them
33 Create
34 Help
35 Making work emails more professional.
36 Nothing of my knowledge.
37 Asking advice and questions about music
38 Word check
39 For brainstorm
40 To help with essay writing, primarily.
41 To help organize my thoughts on a subject
42 I don't normally use it
43 Recipes and coming up with ideas for fitness routine ideas
44 Don't know
45 AI Prompt engineering for work as well as finding sources of research in courses
46 Inspiration to get ideas flowing before doing my own research.
47 Specific searches
48 Help with breaking down steps in an easier manner for math/statistics problems.
49 Learning new concepts
50 For fun
51 Outlines and idea brainstorming
52 Studies
53 Questions that would take too long to research or aren't necessarily worth the time it would take to find the answer
54 For my projects and assignments
55 Studying tool, idea generator
56 Help on math
57 Brainstorming essay ideas when I'm tired.
58 Studying
59 Whenever I'm curious or want to learn something in a somewhat detail explanation ChatGPT my question.
60 Help with outlines for papers
61 I don't think we should be using generative AI. Especially in school.
62 Rephrasing ideas
63 Cooking recipes
64 Short writing assignments, activity planning
65 Outlines for essays and math homework
66 I usually use it to help me summarize studies for my psych class when the material is too dense.

67 Check work, inspiration for projects before doing my own research
68 A faster more direct Google basically. The next generation of search engines.
69 Writing drafts of cover letters, which I can then clean up into my own language.
70 Editing job and club applications and to have topics explained to me (both in and out of school topics)
71 Learning
72 Schoolwork
73 Understanding Concepts
74 Brainstorming; fun
75 Mundane tasks that I need to complete for class. or random questions
76 Generating initial ideas for projects Summarizing long texts & case studies Initial ideas for research
77 Editing essays, writing and debugging code, asking questions that require visiting multiple websites
78 Write
79 School
80 Correct grammar of my text

Fine Arts and Architecture

1 To plan vacations and what to do in certain countries.
2 I sometimes use my computer's copilot ai to answer questions google did not answer very well.
3 More help understanding difficult concepts from class
4 Random life questions
5 Improving graphics
6 Fun
7 To come up with topics
8 Emails, historical information on black people, scriptures & books, artist in America and overseas.
9 Graphics
10 Homework help
11 Nothing
12 I use it for quick summary answers to help solve problems and for proofreading essays to make sure the grammar is right
13 None
14 Information and editing
15 I do not.
16 Help organize tasks
17 Providing sources for topic research and improving the wording in essays
18 Asking questions, creating ideas for art
19 Help with writing
20 To check my spelling and grammar mistakes
21 Nothing
22 Nothing.

23 Coding after effects expressions
24 Writing
25 Condensing my thoughts to get a rough outline and then I rewrite it myself
26 For understanding the current status of what AI can comprehend. Such as, when there are new updates, I would like to know if current events are understood.
27 Grammatical errors
28 Writing
29 Writing ideas
30 Clarify prompts
31 Ideas, I had a class that required us to use Midjourney
32 I don't usually use AI unless for messing around on character AI ever once in a while or if it pops up on Google searches
33 I asked it yesterday to recommend a Starbucks drink for someone who hates coffee. I basically just use it to ask questions that are deeper and require more understanding than google. Like ones I feel google couldn't answer because it isn't a person.
34 summarizing large chunks of text and coming up with topic idea
35 I took an AI class this semester and needed to generate a short film using AI. I used Eggnog AI to generate all those scenes and voices. For my other classes, it reads my writing and points out areas of weakness. This helps me improve areas of my writing that I've overlooked.
36 Outlining essays
37 To help me think of ideas for course work as well as personal projects
38 Checking grammar and spelling mistakes.
39 I don't use it
40 Brainstorming
41 Organizing my schedule
42 For summarizing for compiling information into something much more manageable and time efficient for studying or research. Ex: bullet point lists listing out main ideas in an academic paper or transcribing a YouTube video.
43 Nothing
44 Drafting
45 I try to avoid using generative AI (especially because of the climate impacts)

Music, Dance, Theater, other Performing Arts

1 I use Grammarly to proofread, but that's it.
2 I used ChatGPT like twice to get prompts for a couple of projects
3 Microsoft
4 Research
5 Mostly to play around and see what it says for fun, occasionally use it to help outline assignments but I don't have it write papers for me.
6 Fun
7 Nothing

8 I have used ChatGPT in the past for school assignments
9 Nothing
10 Nothing
11 Spell checking, grammar, random questions that couldn't get answered by google search, learning about different things in the span of 5 minutes.
12 To help me gather intel on certain things, it's easier to ask something that can help me find the answers I'm looking for.
13 Finding good academic sources for papers
14 Help with research and grammar correction.
15 Fun

English, Foreign Languages, Comp Literature, Creative Writing

1 Generate ideas or ask medical questions
2 I do not
3 Chatting
4 I do not use AI applications (beyond the basics of something like a spellcheck implemented in writing software, and even that I don't trust to be accurate)
5 I use them to quickly and accurately summarize information so that I may more easily understand difficult concepts I am learning about. I also use AI to organize an plans things. If I can delegate "grunt work" of my life (for instance scheduling, classwork that isn't relevant to my career, etc.) to AI so that I can focus on my passions then I sometimes do.
6 Data collating
7 1. Getting past learning roadblocks in my self-paced, online, video tutorial-based web design course. I am learning to use Figma, a web design software. Whenever I can't figure something out from the tutorial, I just ask Gemini and the problem is usually resolved in minutes. 2. Internet searches that are more specific.
8 To help brainstorm ideas for my DnD campaign
9 Quick questions that come off the top of my mind. (how old would __ be if...) (kg to lbs.)
10 Brainstorming and revisions
11 Get ideas
12 School work
13 Nothing
14 Quick questions about personal thing I want to know, like shopping, outfit ideas, birthday planning, etc.
15 I don't use them
16 Double check answers or give brainstorming advice
17 Therapy and brainstorming research ideas
18 Finding information
19 Making to do lists, organizing schedules, making practice tests

Biology, Physics, Chemistry, Pre-Med

1 I use it to make my essays better.
2 I use AI for choosing options when I cannot make a decision. I also use it for title ideas and essay outlines.
3 Explaining answers and concepts for my math courses and finishing essays for my English courses.
4 Brainstorming
5 Anything involving math, typically to teach me concepts of a specific problem
6 Help with ideas for papers or for study guides. 80/20 study method too
7 Homework help
8 Homework
9 Reflection and I use it for studying and active recall
10 Help studying and giving me practice tests.
11 Understanding, visualizing, or working through problems. Typically confusing crochet patterns or chemistry problems.
12 To help generate ideas, to search things up rather than using google, to help me come up with synonyms so I sound more professional.
13 Test prep
14 Meal prepping, workouts
15 I use AI to generate quiz or exam questions to practice and study.
16 If I did. writing a paper I don't want to
17 Studying
18 Homework
19 Questions, to form ideas as well as to enhance my writing.
20 Nothing
21 To help me come up with ideas and steer me in the right direction
22 I use it to generate ideas for the assignments and help with brainstorming sessions. I also use it to modify my articles and writing assignments.
23 Studying
24 Study
25 Asking research questions and sometimes cooking recipes.
26 I mostly use AI to decipher information from academic journals and sometimes to refine my writing
27 To answer questions no one around me knows the answer to
28 If I have a question and type it into Google, I will read what the Google AI has summarized, or if there is a problem in my notes I need to have explained.
29 help with minor assignments
30 Nothing
31 I use it like google and to research new topics outside of school
32 Helping me in essays
33 Understanding topics
34 For checking my grammar
35 Asking questions I can't ask people.
36 Help with my homework

37 Reasoning questions
38 Education
39 Grammar Check
40 School and work
41 Coursework
42 Information
43 Helping with studying, researching new topics
44 To generate pictures.
45 Reviewing notes
46 Grammar, rewording of phrases, brain storms, and research
47 Helping with document writing, report preparation, and speeches.
48 Scaffolding outlines or explaining complicated concepts or ideas. This helps me identify my own learning gaps in material. Also summarizing large amounts of text.
49 Efficient learning, problem solving, philosophical pondering
50 I only ever use it for personal projects that I don't care much about and just need something quickly thrown together
51 I don't use it
52 Studying
53 Help with schoolwork
54 School
55 Explaining science concepts in simpler words and asking questions about concepts.
56 To streamline polishing grammatical errors. To help organize thoughts. To assist in planning agendas of personal use.
57 Refining resume and essays
58 Coding(for R for example)
59 Generating ideas for topics/assignments, practice question generation for interviews/resumes/etc.
60 Applications
61 Generating sentences with my Chinese vocab words and finding specific synonyms
62 I primarily use artificial intelligence applications for research, organization, and learning purposes. AI helps me analyze large volumes of information quickly, making it easier to find relevant academic papers, summarize key points, and identify emerging trends. I also use AI tools for writing assistance, including generating drafts, refining my essays, and improving my clarity and structure. Additionally, AI applications support my exploration of complex topics by providing explanations, generating ideas, and helping me brainstorm solutions to challenging problems. It's also been helpful for enhancing creativity, especially in projects related to theater and community engagement.
63 Editing essays/grammar checker
64 School
65 Practice problems, further explaining topics that I don’t understand, brainstorming
66 Breaking down ideas
67 Nothing. They're generally useless or academically damaging in my opinion. They are "efficient," but efficiency doesn't necessarily correlate to

genuine work ethic or genuine understanding of academic concepts and theories.
68 Homework
69 Asking questions - search engine
70 Understanding biology concepts
71 Answering questions I have
72 Ideas for class titles or writing questions
73 To elaborate on information I may not understand
74 To catch minor errors in essays and summarize text for better comprehension
75 The only time I used it was for help with math.
76 Checking calculations, debugging code, explaining sentences in textbook
77 learning and explanations
78 Code syntax help
79 How to structure presentations/ papers and help make my words more concise since I tend to ramble and use more informal language
80 Drafting emails, checking answers to questions I have already done, brainstorming ideas
81 Making emails sound a little better
82 Nothing; I've only used AI two or three times in my life.
83 Questions
84 Reading and illustrating the codes or scripts.

Geology, Oceanography, Environmental Sciences

1 If anything, for generating inspiration or prompts
2 Creative personal projects
3 Mainly to verify answers for course material and random questions
4 I do not typically use them. The only time I ever use AI is when I search something on Google and the Google AI auto generates information at the top of the screen, and I am not using AI on purpose.
5 I've used it on TikTok to make art out of my pictures but that's about it.
6 It occasionally pops up on Google. Although I try to avoid it
7 I do not use them
8 Google forcing it to be the top result
9 I only used AI once, for help in constructing a playlist. It wasn't very helpful.
10 Brainstorming, pasta on the wall, checking grammar & flow of emails
11 I oppose generative AI on personal and ethical grounds. I used it once to translate a Korean poem that had no English translation available, but that's it. I consider the use of AI to be like consulting a classmate without the benefits of actual peer support— convenient but opens you up to misinformation and plagiarism risk. I predict that I will have to use non-generative AI in my professional work, but I don't believe that I will ever need generative AI, so I have not prioritized developing the skill. I am also concerned about the socioeconomic and environmental effects of the AI

industry. Lastly, I am not convinced that I will be sufficiently protected by the data privacy policies of some of these applications.
12 Answering questions that I don't know how to answer
13 Writing

Engineering, Mathematics, Computer Science

1 Nothing
2 None
3 Research and templates
4 Studying
5 Ask random questions especially when I can't get straight answers on google
6 Study plans and practice problems.
7 Help with writing.
8 For writing assignments "grading"
9 Coursework
10 To help me with course work. It is very useful to clarify concepts and guide you through exercises on mathematics or statistics.
11 I use it to get detailed information about topics if google does not give me the details I need
12 To ask questions, summarize web info, suggestion on general life .
13 Generating ideas for projects, whether personal or coursework related. Brainstorming.
14 Learning and Development
15 Checking mathematical proofs and models.
16 School
17 Answer small question
18 Ideas on how to compose letters or writings
19 Providing context behind certain topics, brief fact checks, feedback for personal hobbies
20 General questions to narrow down
21 For academic purposes and programming and coding different software tools.
22 I do not use generative AI. The only AI I am aware of using is that used in the background of current Android phones for energy management. Machine learning programs are a different matter, though I do not frequently use them outside of integrated applications.
23 Clarification and correction
24 School
25 If I were to, help on a solution or to start brainstorming a project
26 Math
27 Research, code examples
28 Workshopping Grammar, Citing/ Finding sources
29 I use ChatGPT if I want to dive deeper into a topic I've talk about in class especially if the teacher wasn't clear in teaching and was being vague
30 For education
31 Research

32 Initial and primarily for assignments that required it however it does help understand things or give alternative perspective in stuff I'm trying to figure out
33 Learning
34 Entertainment
35 AI modelling, Machine learning
36 Learning, coding assistance
37 Making and building projects , portfolios
38 To outline the project ideas
39 Help with homework
40 Help with homework and answering specific questions I have that a simple Google search might not do the trick.
41 Recipes Travel Planning
42 Correcting my writing and checking for errors in my equations for math homework
43 For some help with generating ideas.
44 Just to mess around with
45 Look up any quick answering questions in my free time and guide me to write an essay format with paragraph examples.
46 Create images or ask for advice of social relationships
47 Homework, explaining how to perform a task, research, sources, citation generator (easyBib has too many ads)
48 Assignment
49 Don't use it
50 To help me with my study and sometimes for general purposes.
51 Education
52 Not sure
53 It's a powerful tool. I use it to help me with childcare questions, mental health questions, academic questions, and even relationship advice.
54 Brainstorming
55 Learning the basics of specific topics
56 Questions I have
57 Learning more information about subjects/topics in my courses and as a place to write out my thoughts while having something respond
58 I avoid them.
59 Ideas to start difficult problems, usually in math
60 I use it to organize information and to define terms or code snippets to better understand them.
61 Brainstorming, putting ideas in order; like an interactive journal
62 for a bit of information
63 Explaining concepts that a textbook doesn't explain clearly.
64 Summarizing slides/lecture notes provided by professors
65 Understanding homework problems, diagnosing issues with my code
66 Learning, I self-study a lot so it makes it much easier to deconstruct challenging concepts
67 Helping to understand notes, better explain textbook and in class examples, and generate and grade practice exams to assist in studying.
68 Summarizing complex articles, understanding new things
69 Do university stuff.

70 Help with coursework
71 Understand subjects that I struggle with better
72 As a search engine, since they filter out any sponsored results from Google
73 Studying and learning about topics I need more help on
74 Starting to outline ideas
75 If I need more information about a topic
76 Learning and Questioning
77 Coursework
78 Research/schoolwork
79 Improving essays
80 This semester (technically not this month) I used it for assignments to generate sample practice quiz questions for my programming methodology class.
81 Questions that won't have a straightforward answer on Google
82 Nothing
83 Making plans, researching basic topics, saving time
84 For problem-solving
85 Research, Studying and Home works
86 For Research
87 Homework assignments
88 Ideas
89 Learning
90 Homework essays, email responses
91 Homework help
92 Information summary and synthesis, a bit of fun
93 School work, self-development, ADHD help to break down tasks
94 Mental health support, application help, academic support
95 Helping make study guides
96 Psychological support, schoolwork, job work and applications, info seeking, and random questions.
97 Clarity in work and more perspectives to issues
98 For school and coding
99 To give me feedback on my work, in order to improve my essays. I also ask it questions which Google has a harder time answering
100 Mainly daily questions such as "what shirt size should I buy (assuming it's a Chinese chart)" and "can I recycle ..."
101 Reviewing concepts missed during coursework
102 Learning tool
103 Help with coding for personal engineering projects
104 Grammar checking and quick technical definition lookups / explanations.
105 I mainly use it to check my work on math problems and to explain confusing concepts in both math and chemistry.
106 Helping explain stuff to me
107 Help with homework
108 Summarizing ideas, suggesting edits for my writing, summarizing my essays to ensure I get the point I am trying to across, debugging code, suggesting problem solving steps

109 Brainstorming ideas; summarizing concepts or information
110 Writing advice
111 Quickly summarize large chunks of text, or to get a quick answer to a very tedious but uncomplicated problem
112 To help provide me information and evidence on topics/arguments and to come up with ideas in support of what I prompt it.
113 Explaining things in more detail
114 Help on homework usually, to explain concepts, do my citations, or help me make notes and proofread papers
115 Everything
116 Teaching academic material and making career searching more efficient
117 Resume/CV writing
118 homework guidance
119 summarizing information, getting a quick intro to certain topics, brainstorming ideas
120 Help drafting text to then edit manually for emails, LinkedIn requests, etc.
121 Learning
122 Background research and assistance during coding
123 I asked ChatGPT to make me a marathon training schedule once and then I asked it to explain why I got a homework answer wrong but other than that I really don't use it
124 Programming, data visualizations and analysis for research, HW, to refine my writing.
125 Replacement search engine, adapting to unfamiliar Apis, recipes, confirming validity of translations, answering weird specific questions of no consequence
126 Brainstorming
127 Polishing essays, help with assignments, asking for ideas
128 To rephrase stuff to a more suited language
129 Coming up with better adjectives, helping me write application questions
130 Ideas for lesson planning
131 Checking problem set answers
132 Everything
133 Writing software
134 Many things, from personal to professional
135 Advancing my knowledge in my career in civil engineering.
136 For chatting. Getting information in an informal way.
137 Homework help

History, Classics

1 I only use what comes up in a search and I only use it peripherally.
2 To summarize comments on Facebook or an article I'm reading
3 lifestyle stuff, creating meal plans for my weeks, creating exercise routines, and store lists
4 Coding, compiling lists, edits, google search engine

5 Help with coding in R for a class (that I've now finished)
6 Help with code in RStudio. But the class is now over.
7 I don't use AI applications
8 Checking my grammar, asking for advice on the tone of an email

Sociology, Political Science, Anthropology or other Social Science, except Economics and Psychology

1 Help with homework/simplify readings
2 research
3 Most of the time it's used to rephrase questions from assignments in simpler terms, or for grammar checks.
4 I don't
5 I use AI for Duolingo, television, and phone games. I do not use AI for schoolwork besides the Google search engine.
6 Generating pictures of the characters in my novel.
7 Coursework
8 I use it for a variety of activities, but primarily I use it for academic purposes and for language study.
9 Grammar check
10 I do not use it.
11 Routines and schedule goals
12 General information
13 Editing and proofreading, verifying sources
14 It just butts in, so sometimes I'll skim for sources. Primarily I don't use it.
15 To know about any questions
16 Breaking down and explaining concepts
17 Bibliography format check,
18 Ideas, checking, rewording, resources
19 Scheduling, meal prep, summaries, writing of biographies, study plan formulation
20 Helping me write texts
21 Ideas
22 Help with writing assignments
23 Automation and Task Managing
24 Improving argumentative writing by asking for an array of questions.
25 Studying
26 Summaries, providing a better way to say something or general analysis
27 Help with writing, help with coding.
28 Finding information, relevant academic articles, get a rough idea of the project, making process charts etc.
29 Educational research
30 Summarizing, sparking thought process
31 Writing resume/ cover letter/ emails
32 Finding sources or if I have a quick question.
33 Study tools, draft emails and general search engine

34 Summarizing readings, brainstorming ideas, formulating professional email responses, rewording sentences
35 Organization of ideas, especially mindless tasks like drafting email responses and routines.
36 Class, personal relationships, style advice, honestly almost everything I'm confused about
37 Summarizing text, cleaning up notes
38 Occasionally I use it to brainstorm ideas or construct outlines when it's allowed, but I don't use it to write.
39 Personal things
40 Search engine
41 I use it for curiosity. For example, I ask historical questions I might have, and I do not have a book on the topic to learn about it.
42 Ask philosophical question to see what the ai's view are or just ask them questions I have
43 Research, historical context
44 My primary use of AI is to aid me in combating ADHD and facilitating my life through simplification, for example writing emails, discussing class notes, getting out of depressive ruts, etc.
45 I don't use it
46 Schoolwork
47 I don't really use it. Sometimes to formulate sentences or ideas I am stuck with

Psychology

1 Help correcting my essays
2 Nothing
3 Homework
4 I primarily use artificial intelligence applications to help organize and plan for personal goals or staying organized with my coursework. For example, asking AI to create a template so I can upload my class syllabus and reference it easier.
5 In the past I have used ChatGPT to check for spelling errors in my writing, or to find synonyms to certain words.
6 None
7 For fun
8 questions about life or medical conditions
9 I do not use AI
10 Ask for more guidance/ elaboration
11 Help with homework
12 I don't use it
13 Research
14 Nothing.
15 Idea generation
16 I have ADHD and really struggle with mapping out writing assignments, especially long and/or complex ones. I use Claude as a tool to help me organize my thoughts and create paper outlines/maps.
17 General questions

18 Nothing
19 Nothing
20 When I need things explained to me in an easier to understand way. Or, when I need an idea for a project, I can ask ChatGPT to give me a list of starting ideas relevant to my project.
21 Not applicable
22 I would like to use it for help with writing papers
23 Collecting info
24 I don't use it
25 Making workout plans, getting life advice
26 Editing pictures
27 Help on essays
28 For fun
29 I use AI for general questions and curiosities.
30 Summarizing academic papers, searching for and querying about said papers
31 I don't like to use AI for my tasks and don't plan to in the future if I can help it.
32 Locating places, correcting grammar, GPS
33 Checking, finding resources and links, formatting bibliography, helping me find info for titles, ideas, and sometimes a 1 to 2 paragraph taster on some idea I have.
34 Just playing around with them
35 Asking homework questions.
36 When I google something it pops up at the top so I will glance at it and if it's all I need I won't continue my search.
37 How to: e.g., Run SPSS tests
38 Knowledge
39 Never used
40 I don't use them currently
41 None
42 I don't usually use it. I have tested it out on Microsoft. The subscription cost money that I do not have.
43 For creating study guides, generating ideas, my physical and mental health (whoop)
44 I mostly use AI applications for things like helping with writing, answering questions, and sometimes even for fun stuff like generating creative ideas.
45 Ideas for creative writing and questions I have.
46 Fact check myself on topics and to learn more in depth on what I am researching.
47 I use AI for ideas to joke around with people and almost like therapeutic help. I understand it's not an actual replacement for therapy, but it helps sometimes to have a logical perspective.
48 Ideas, outlines
49 Helping with understanding questions
50 To understand assignment
51 Learning, expanding on lectures, etc.

52 Personal use such as meal planning or guided workouts, outlines or organizing academic papers
53 Help create study guides and to also explain complex theories/perspectives that I have trouble understanding
54 Answering general questions
55 Entertainment
56 Writing, excel formulas
57 Information
58 Gaining more knowledge and ideas about certain topics.
59 To clarify notions or ideas, get guidance in personal health problems. Also, to get fast information on niche topics (although there could be some improvement, here, overall).
60 Use it when helping complete assignments but also when in class with the instructors.
61 Ideas, understanding definitions
62 For answers to questions I don't understand, or just to clarify what I'm saying in an essay.
63 Ask questions about daily life
64 To explain processes I don't understand
65 I don't.
66 Answering my questions, generating ideas for things, finding good synonyms, re-phrasing sentences.
67 Meal prep ideas, bedtime story ideas
68 Questions- academic and personal, revising, editing
69 A class had us use it to code in R.
70 To get advice about my life
71 Ideation
72 Math/code help and writing emails
73 School help

Education or Library Science

1 When I need to find a word for something specific
2 Ideas
3 I don't
4 Help with harder questions to build better understanding
5 To help fix writing and grammar mistakes
6 To see the steps for solving a problem or to help with grammar
7 Dumb images
8 Nothing.
9 I don't use it
10 Email templates.
11 New ideas for lesson plans
12 Clarifying emails
13 Study questions philosophy questions and sometimes if I just need to journal
14 Writing music
15 To check spelling
16 None

17 Homework answers
18 Ideas for educational activities for students or help creating worksheets and instructional materials.
19 Several of my homework assignments have required the use of AI technology in order to create lesson plan templates, simplify the Ohio Education Standards, and other creative practices utilized in the educational field. I have also used ChatGPT as guidance in my research, Alexa to answer miscellaneous questions, and when using Google or Facebook, an AI generated response is often created to simplify my search.
20 Better understanding on topics I don't fully understand at first
21 Help with outlines, helping talk about my feelings, answering random specific questions that google didn't understand
22 Lesson planning and teaching resources.
23 Writing, research
24 Revising essays.
25 Idea generation in writing essays
26 I don't.
27 I use it to check my answers and my grammar.
28 Alleviate boredom or to help generate or outline ideas for writing
29 Help revising my work
30 Grammar and spelling check
31 Nothing
32 To help proofread and to help organize my brainstormed ideas.
33 Don't use any
34 Research and sometimes.
35 Personally, I use ChatGPT for all my everyday questions. Just like I used to ask Google a million and one questions back in the day when it first came out (and Jeeves before that), I now ask ChatGPT. Professionally, I use MagicSchool AI a lot because it helps with creating lesson plans, adapting reading assignments, writing assignments, and crafting emails/letters to parents.
36 I use ai as a copy editor for papers and to help generate first drafts of work emails.
37 Help with studying
38 I look up help in social media captions
39 Research and inspirations
40 To come up with ideas for lesson plans. as a future teacher, I'm required to come up with countless lesson plans and I use ai to help me come up with ideas and activities to include in the lesson plans
41 To double check my grammar mainly, and sometimes to help smoothly transition sentences in essays.
42 Understanding the wording of online coursework
43 I used ChatGPT to help me draft cover letters for job applications
44 Revising professional communication with peers and clients.
45 I don't
46 Rewriting, grammar, and lengthening
47 Generating ideas, wording for emails
48 Edit occasional emails.

Criminology/Law Enforcement

1 Finding specific answers to things when Google doesn't give me a good one.
2 Nothing, I'm against AI
3 I don't use artificial intelligence, but I do have a LinkedIn subscription as it helps me know what jobs would be best for me to apply for and understand if my resume aligns with certain job descriptions
4 Liner or ChatGPT
5 self help
6 Getting information quickly
7 Nothing. I do not use generative AI.
8 Spell checking
9 Never used
10 Math
11 Looking for quick answers, trying to find research

Occupational or Physical Therapy, Nursing, Public Health, Nutrition. other Health-Related

1 I don't use it
2 Homework
3 Study
4 I don't know
5 To get me started on essays
6 Answer questions fast.
7 Learning material I do not fully comprehend my professors explanations to.
8 School work
9 Looking up in depth information
10 research, entertainment, random web surfing, and niche interests
11 Basic questions, homework, recipes. Pretty much anything I used to use google for.
12 Helping with math problems and summarizing articles
13 To learn more about coursework, ask more in depth questions, help with specific assignments/ questions about math problems
14 Explanations in topics I do not understand on my own
15 Explanations in topics I do not understand on my own
16 Help with class work and better understanding of new things
17 Trying to dumb down complex information that I need to know that we talked about in classes but I don't remember.
18 Nothing
19 To help find words similar to other words to exact the thought I'm thinking of
20 School
21 Making funny pictures
22 Writings, answers for my questions instead of google search engine
23 Generating structural ideas for papers
24 Understanding concepts and quizzing self

25 Outlining my ideas
26 I'll use it for YouTube video ideas or to help fix my resume or identity bugs and animals
27 Questions
28 Help answer questions
29 Used for a nursing informatics assignment
30 Citations Proofreading Outline generation
31 Studying, if you give it your notes or test content it can generate questions.
32 Entertainment
33 Further explanation for topics talked over in class or questions I may have
34 Symptoms I may have or an answer in everyday living that I may need.
35 To explain things I don't understand.
36 To check my gramma or the general flow of my work.
37 Guidance on where to start with assignments and answering longer questions
38 Some school work
39 Better understand topics. It will break the main topic down for me.
40 Nothing
41 Coming up with problem examples to help me understand the material
42 When I'm stumped by chemistry questions after trying to solve them.
43 Most people use it to help them study
44 Emails, Prep questions? Studying, Brainstorming, grammar
45 Answers to quick questions
46 Curiosity
47 To provide templates for certain documents, google searches, or whenever I am seeking additional information on a specific topic/idea.
48 Day-to-day activities, School work
49 Forming emails
50 Question.
51 Outlines for papers, understanding a concept, studying for tests
52 To find out more information on books I read or just to vent about what I have going on in life
53 Nothing
54 As a replacement for google
55 Study help
56 Questions in research that I am unsure about
57 Help look up information
58 I have used it once to get book recommendations
59 School ideas
60 Google searches.
61 Nothing
62 Personal
63 For nursing school study tool
64 Nothing

65 I don't currently use
66 Tutoring, math, vocab
67 Writing reference letters
68 Ideas
69 Creating presentations
70 Studying
71 Fleshing out ideas or starting points to projects.
72 I use it for suggestions on the best methods for completing DIY projects, helping to plan out timed tasks effectively, and refining my writing in important communications and cards, among other things.
73 Paper outlines
74 Rewording sentence structure and creating templates.
75 Homework answers
76 Research, document drafting and proofing

Communications, Media, Journalism

1 I don't use it
2 Help with paper idea's.
3 To help me come up with creative titles for non-school related work or to help me answer questions I have about things.
4 Help me brainstorm ideas
5 To learn more about something.
6 Film editing assistance. Masking, sky replacement, subject remover.
7 To look younger on photographs!!!
8 Nothing
9 Photoshop
10 I don't use any artificial intelligence applications.
11 As an academic support and general questions
12 Research
13 help with work
14 Food ideas, school questions
15 Research and formatting.
16 Checking my work or understanding for my online classes
17 Summarization, Idea generation

Other

1 Questions I have
2 In rare cases, mixed media art additives and ideas.
3 Fun. I just like to goof around on them.
4 To research and verify information
5 If anything, I use it for short term entertainment with my friends or when I need an image for comedic effect in something sarcastic.
6 I never use AI applications
7 Brainstorm
8 Nothing

## Table 6.1 When you conduct general internet searches. about what percentage of the time do you use a generative AI application to accompany or fully replace your usual search engine?

| | Mean | Median | Minimum | Maximum |
|---|---|---|---|---|
| Entire sample | 25.17 | 10.00 | 0.00 | 100.00 |

## Table 6.2 When you conduct general internet searches, about what percentage of the time do you use a generative AI application to accompany or fully replace your usual search engine? Broken out by tuition of college attended

| Tuition of college attended | Mean | Median | Minimum | Maximum |
|---|---|---|---|---|
| Less than $6,000 | 21.73 | 10.00 | 0.00 | 100.00 |
| $6,000+ - $12,000 | 23.47 | 10.00 | 0.00 | 100.00 |
| $12,000+ - $20,000 | 28.56 | 20.00 | 0.00 | 100.00 |
| More than $20,000 | 27.09 | 20.00 | 0.00 | 100.00 |

## Table 6.3 When you conduct general internet searches, about what percentage of the time do you use a generative AI application to accompany or fully replace your usual search engine? Broken out by enrollment of college attended

| Enrollment of college attended | Mean | Median | Minimum | Maximum |
|---|---|---|---|---|
| Less than 5,000 | 26.66 | 20.00 | 0.00 | 100.00 |
| 5,000+ - 12,000 | 26.23 | 20.00 | 0.00 | 100.00 |
| 12,000+ - 22,900 | 26.17 | 10.00 | 0.00 | 100.00 |
| More than 22,900 | 22.16 | 10.00 | 0.00 | 100.00 |

## Table 6.4 When you conduct general internet searches, about what percentage of the time do you use a generative AI application to accompany or fully replace your usual search engine? Broken out by public or private college

| Public or private college | Mean | Median | Minimum | Maximum |
|---|---|---|---|---|
| Public | 24.50 | 10.00 | 0.00 | 100.00 |
| Private | 27.42 | 20.00 | 0.00 | 100.00 |

## Table 6.5 When you conduct general internet searches, about what percentage of the time do you use a generative AI application to accompany or fully replace your usual search engine? Broken out by age of respondent

| Age of respondent | Mean | Median | Minimum | Maximum |
|---|---|---|---|---|
| Under 19 | 25.22 | 10.00 | 0.00 | 100.00 |
| 19-21 | 25.58 | 20.00 | 0.00 | 100.00 |
| 22-27 | 27.59 | 20.00 | 0.00 | 100.00 |
| Over 28 | 21.60 | 10.00 | 0.00 | 100.00 |

## Table 6.6 When you conduct general internet searches, about what percentage of the time do you use a generative AI application to accompany or fully replace your usual search engine? Broken out by urban, suburban or rural upbringing

| Urban, suburban or rural upbringing | Mean | Median | Minimum | Maximum |
|---|---|---|---|---|
| I grew up in a major city with more than 350,000 people | 27.21 | 15.00 | 0.00 | 100.00 |
| I grew up in a small or medium sized city with less than 350,000 people. | 28.30 | 20.00 | 0.00 | 100.00 |
| I grew up in a suburban area | 21.82 | 10.00 | 0.00 | 100.00 |
| I grew up in a rural area. | 23.15 | 10.00 | 0.00 | 100.00 |
| Unknown | 50.00 | 50.00 | 50.00 | 50.00 |

## Table 6.7 When you conduct general internet searches, about what percentage of the time do you use a generative AI application to accompany or fully replace your usual search engine? Broken out by region of upbringing

| Region of upbringing | Mean | Median | Minimum | Maximum |
|---|---|---|---|---|
| The South | 26.64 | 20.00 | 0.00 | 100.00 |
| The Northeast | 25.26 | 16.25 | 0.00 | 100.00 |
| The Midwest | 19.57 | 8.50 | 0.00 | 100.00 |
| The West | 25.83 | 20.00 | 0.00 | 100.00 |
| Abroad | 38.18 | 37.50 | 0.00 | 100.00 |

## Table 6.8 When you conduct general internet searches, about what percentage of the time do you use a generative AI application to accompany or fully replace your usual search engine? Broken out by year of class standing

| Year of class standing | Mean | Median | Minimum | Maximum |
|---|---|---|---|---|
| First year student | 26.32 | 15.00 | 0.00 | 100.00 |
| Sophomore | 22.63 | 10.00 | 0.00 | 100.00 |
| Junior | 24.24 | 15.00 | 0.00 | 100.00 |
| Senior | 25.93 | 10.00 | 0.00 | 100.00 |
| Unknown | 30.00 | 17.50 | 10.00 | 75.00 |

## Table 6.9 When you conduct general internet searches, about what percentage of the time do you use a generative AI application to accompany or fully replace your usual search engine? Broken out by annual family of origin income level

| Annual family of origin income level | Mean | Median | Minimum | Maximum |
|---|---|---|---|---|
| Less than $50,000 per year | 29.28 | 20.00 | 0.00 | 100.00 |
| $50,000 to $90,000 per year | 24.22 | 15.00 | 0.00 | 100.00 |
| $90,000+ to $150,000 per year | 20.81 | 10.00 | 0.00 | 90.00 |
| $150,000+ to $250,000 per year | 21.18 | 10.00 | 0.00 | 80.00 |
| More than $250,000 per year | 32.98 | 20.00 | 0.00 | 100.00 |
| Unknown | 11.25 | 10.00 | 5.00 | 20.00 |

## Table 6.10 When you conduct general internet searches, about what percentage of the time do you use a generative AI application to accompany or fully replace your usual search engine? Broken out by relationship with organized religion

| Relationship with organized religion | Mean | Median | Minimum | Maximum |
|---|---|---|---|---|
| I practice a religion thoroughly and consider my religion to be a very important part of my life. | 24.26 | 20.00 | 0.00 | 100.00 |
| I practice a religion and try to attend regular services and to participate as much as I can. | 21.31 | 10.00 | 0.00 | 95.00 |
| I identify with a religion but can't say I put a lot of effort into practicing it. | 29.92 | 20.00 | 0.00 | 95.00 |
| I don't really believe in or practice an organized religion. | 23.81 | 5.50 | 0.00 | 100.00 |
| Unknown | 45.00 | 45.00 | 30.00 | 60.00 |

## Table 6.11 When you conduct general internet searches, what percentage of the time do you use a generative AI application to accompany or fully replace your usual search engine? Broken out by political views

| Political views | Mean | Median | Minimum | Maximum |
|---|---|---|---|---|
| Very left wing | 16.09 | 0.00 | 0.00 | 100.00 |
| Liberal | 26.97 | 15.00 | 0.00 | 100.00 |
| Middle of the road | 26.38 | 11.25 | 0.00 | 100.00 |
| Conservative | 24.70 | 20.00 | 0.00 | 93.00 |
| Very right wing | 41.54 | 30.00 | 0.00 | 100.00 |
| Unknown | 45.00 | 45.00 | 45.00 | 45.00 |

## Table 6.12 When you conduct general internet searches, about what percentage of the time do you use a generative AI application to accompany or fully replace your usual search engine? Broken out by college grades

| College grades | Mean | Median | Minimum | Maximum |
|---|---|---|---|---|
| A or A- average or more | 24.67 | 10.00 | 0.00 | 100.00 |
| B or B+ average | 26.35 | 15.00 | 0.00 | 100.00 |
| C or C+ or lower | 25.30 | 20.00 | 0.00 | 100.00 |

## Table 6.13 When you conduct general internet searches, about what percentage of the time do you use a generative AI application to accompany or fully replace your usual search engine? Broken out by academic major

| Academic major | Mean | Median | Minimum | Maximum |
|---|---|---|---|---|
| Business, Economics or Finance | 27.76 | 15.00 | 0.00 | 100.00 |
| Psychology | 28.39 | 10.00 | 0.00 | 100.00 |
| Education or Library Science | 15.64 | 5.00 | 0.00 | 70.00 |
| Criminology/Law Enforcement | 15.71 | 0.00 | 0.00 | 60.00 |
| Occupational or Physical Therapy, Nursing, Public Health, Nutrition. other Health-Related | 30.64 | 25.00 | 0.00 | 90.00 |
| Communications, Media, Journalism | 25.45 | 20.00 | 0.00 | 95.00 |
| Fine Arts and Architecture | 17.11 | 0.00 | 0.00 | 100.00 |
| Music, Dance, Theater, other Performing Arts | 21.50 | 0.00 | 0.00 | 100.00 |
| English, Foreign Languages, Comp Literature, Creative Writing | 10.53 | 5.50 | 0.00 | 40.00 |
| Biology, Physics, Chemistry, Pre-Med | 32.20 | 30.00 | 0.00 | 95.00 |
| Geology, Oceanography, Environmental Sciences | 2.85 | 0.00 | 0.00 | 20.00 |
| Engineering, Mathematics, Computer Science | 26.29 | 20.00 | 0.00 | 100.00 |
| History, Classics | 27.50 | 5.00 | 0.00 | 100.00 |
| Sociology, Political Science, Anthropology or other Social Science, except Economics and Psychology | 25.66 | 20.00 | 0.00 | 100.00 |
| Other | 17.19 | 2.50 | 0.00 | 75.00 |

## Table 6.14 When you conduct general internet searches, about what percentage of the time do you use a generative AI application to accompany or fully replace your usual search engine? Broken out by gender of respondent

| Gender of respondent | Mean | Median | Minimum | Maximum |
|---|---|---|---|---|
| Male | 26.60 | 15.00 | 0.00 | 100.00 |
| Female | 25.61 | 10.25 | 0.00 | 100.00 |
| Transgender | 13.74 | 0.00 | 0.00 | 100.00 |
| Unknown | 1.00 | 1.00 | 1.00 | 1.00 |

## Table 6.15 When you conduct general internet searches, about what percentage of the time do you use a generative AI application to accompany or fully replace your usual search engine? Broken out by status of current residency

| Status of current residency | Mean | Median | Minimum | Maximum |
|---|---|---|---|---|
| At home with my parents or guardian | 27.11 | 20.00 | 0.00 | 100.00 |
| Off campus with others who are not my parents or guardian | 27.71 | 15.00 | 0.00 | 100.00 |
| Off campus alone | 23.13 | 10.00 | 0.00 | 100.00 |
| On campus in the dorms or college-provided suites | 23.44 | 10.00 | 0.00 | 100.00 |
| Unknown | 0.00 | 0.00 | 0.00 | 0.00 |

## Table 6.16 When you conduct general internet searches, about what percentage of the time do you use a generative AI application to accompany or fully replace your usual search engine? Broken out by current employment situation

| Current employment situation | Mean | Median | Minimum | Maximum |
|---|---|---|---|---|
| I don't have a full or part time job. | 28.63 | 20.00 | 0.00 | 100.00 |
| I have a part time job. | 24.38 | 15.00 | 0.00 | 100.00 |
| I have a full time job. | 19.36 | 5.00 | 0.00 | 100.00 |
| Unknown | 0.00 | 0.00 | 0.00 | 0.00 |

## Table 6.17 When you conduct general internet searches, about what percentage of the time do you use a generative AI application to accompany or fully replace your usual search engine? Broken out by sexual orientation

| Sexual orientation | Mean | Median | Minimum | Maximum |
|---|---|---|---|---|
| Heterosexual or "straight" | 26.43 | 20.00 | 0.00 | 100.00 |
| Homosexual or "gay" | 20.71 | 3.00 | 0.00 | 100.00 |
| Bi-sexual | 22.20 | 5.00 | 0.00 | 100.00 |
| Unknown | 34.00 | 50.00 | 0.00 | 50.00 |

## Table 6.18 When you conduct general internet searches, about what percentage of the time do you use a generative AI application to accompany or fully replace your usual search engine? Broken out by SAT or ACT score

| SAT or ACT score | Mean | Median | Minimum | Maximum |
|---|---|---|---|---|
| 30 or over ACT or 1350 or over SAT | 22.52 | 10.00 | 0.00 | 100.00 |
| 24-29 ACT or 1170 to 1349 SAT | 23.09 | 10.00 | 0.00 | 100.00 |
| 20-23 ACT or 1050 to 1169 SAT | 26.51 | 15.00 | 0.00 | 95.00 |
| 17-19 ACT or 900 to 1050 SAT | 29.90 | 25.00 | 0.00 | 100.00 |
| 16 or Under ACT or Under 900 SAT | 32.10 | 3.50 | 0.00 | 99.00 |
| Never took either test | 28.68 | 20.00 | 0.00 | 100.00 |
| Unknown | 13.50 | 15.00 | 0.00 | 20.00 |

## Table 6.19 When you conduct general internet searches, about what percentage of the time do you use a generative AI application to accompany or fully replace your usual search engine? Broken out by race or ethnicity

| Race or ethnicity | Mean | Median | Minimum | Maximum |
|---|---|---|---|---|
| White or Caucasian | 22.76 | 10.00 | 0.00 | 100.00 |
| Black or African American | 24.79 | 20.00 | 0.00 | 100.00 |
| Latino or Hispanic | 31.34 | 20.00 | 0.00 | 100.00 |
| Asian or Asian American | 31.49 | 20.00 | 0.00 | 100.00 |
| American Indigenous, Eskimo, Pacific Islander, Hawaiian Native | 11.25 | 10.00 | 0.00 | 25.00 |
| Mixed race | 22.38 | 10.00 | 0.00 | 100.00 |
| Unknown | 21.67 | 15.00 | 0.00 | 50.00 |

## Table 6.20 When you conduct general internet searches, what percentage of the time do you use a generative AI application to accompany or fully replace your usual search engine? Broken out by religion

| Religion | Mean | Median | Minimum | Maximum |
|---|---|---|---|---|
| I do not practice or identify with an organized religion | 24.25 | 10.00 | 0.00 | 100.00 |
| Hinduism | 33.38 | 20.00 | 0.00 | 90.00 |
| Islam | 36.06 | 35.00 | 0.00 | 99.00 |
| Judaism | 37.50 | 37.50 | 0.00 | 80.00 |
| Mormon | 45.00 | 40.00 | 0.00 | 100.00 |
| Catholic | 24.64 | 20.00 | 0.00 | 95.00 |
| Lutheran | 18.13 | 5.00 | 0.00 | 70.00 |
| Baptist | 18.43 | 2.30 | 0.00 | 100.00 |
| Evangelical Protestant Christianity | 23.61 | 20.00 | 0.00 | 95.00 |
| Protestant Christianity | 29.57 | 30.00 | 0.00 | 93.00 |
| Orthodox Christianity | 27.50 | 17.50 | 5.00 | 85.00 |
| Buddhism | 24.66 | 10.00 | 0.00 | 80.00 |
| Non-Denominational Christianity | 22.27 | 10.00 | 0.00 | 95.00 |
| Other | 26.58 | 10.00 | 0.00 | 100.00 |

www.ingramcontent.com/pod-product-compliance
Lightning Source LLC
LaVergne TN
LVHW080049210926
848481LV00011B/3306